The abcs of Quality Child Care

Dedication

I dedicate this book to my father, Rubens Dos Santos, and to my mother, Jece D. Santos. Thanks for your love and the hard work you endured through the years to give me a better beginning in life.

To my husband and best friend, Rickey, and to my adorable son, Ruben Edwin. I love you both so very much.

Join us on the web at
EarlyChildEd.delmar.com

The 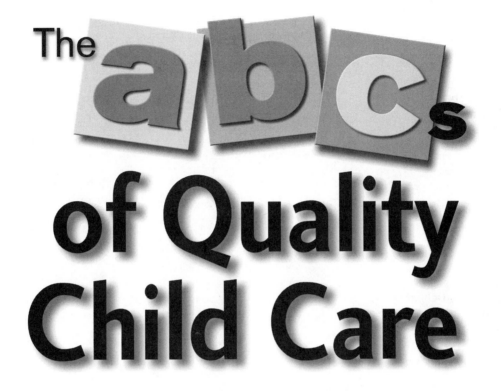 abcs
of Quality
Child Care

Aida Maria Clark

THOMSON

DELMAR LEARNING

Australia Canada Mexico Singapore Spain United Kingdom United States

THOMSON

DELMAR LEARNING™

The ABC's of Quality Child Care
Aida Maria Clark

Business Unit Executive Director:
Susan L. Simpfenderfer

Acquisitions Editor:
Erin O'Connor

Executive Production Manager:
Wendy A. Troeger

Production Editor:
Joy Kocsis

Technology Project Manager:
Joseph Saba

Executive Marketing Manager:
Donna J. Lewis

Channel Manager:
Nigar Hale

Cover Design:
Joseph Villanova

Composition:
Publisher's Studio/
Stratford Publishing Services

For permission to use material from this text or product, contact us by
Tel   (800) 730-2214
Fax   (800) 730-2215
www.thomsonrights.com

Library of Congress Cataloging-in-Publication Data

Clark, Aida Maria.
   The ABC's of quality child care / Aida Maria Clark.
      p. cm.
   Includes index.
   ISBN 1-40180-466-7
   1. Day care centers. 2. Child care services. 3. Child care. I. Title.

   HQ778.5 .C585 2002
   362.71'2--dc21

                                        2002022513

NOTICE TO THE READER

Publisher does not warrant or guarantee any of the products described herein or perform any independent analysis in connection with any of the product information contained herein. Publisher does not assume, and expressly disclaims, any obligation to obtain and include information other than that provided to it by the manufacturer.

The reader is expressly warned to consider and adopt all safety precautions that might be indicated by the activities herein and to avoid all potential hazards. By following the instructions contained herein, the reader willingly assumes all risks in connection with such instructions.

The Publisher makes no representation or warranties of any kind, including but not limited to, the warranties of fitness for particular purpose or merchantability, nor are any such representations implied with respect to the material set forth herein, and the publisher takes no responsibility with respect to such material. The publisher shall not be liable for any special, consequential, or exemplary damages resulting, in whole or part, from the readers' use of, or reliance upon, this material.

Contents

Chapter 3   Safety

Chapter 4   Health

Chapter 5   Schedules and Routines

Chapter 11   **The Role of a Caregiver**

Appendixes

Big Wishes for a Successful Beginning!

First, let me congratulate you for the greatly rewarding career you have chosen to pursue. It is my pleasure to welcome you to the child care business!

As you probably know, child care is in great demand today. With the increasing numbers of both parents working outside of their homes to support their families, child care has become a great area of concern. Left with the guilt of leaving their children for long periods of time and the responsibility of finding the best care possible for their children, parents want to find quality child care programs and responsive caregivers, that will appropriately care for their children.

I know that if you are reading this book right now, you have the best intentions to be and do your utmost for the benefit of children. Taking the time to learn what children need to grow and develop with confidence and success is the first step you need to take to provide children with positive learning experiences.

I wish you the best! I know that with time, effort, and knowledge you will be able to give the children in your care the best beginning in life. Children are counting on you!

The author and Delmar Learning affirm that the Web site URLs referenced herein were accurate at the time of printing. However, due to the fluid nature of the Internet, we cannot guarantee their accuracy for the life of the edition.

Online Resources™

The Online Resources™ to accompany *The ABC's of Quality Child Care* is your link to early childhood education on the Internet. The Online Resources™ contain many features to help focus your understanding of quality child care:

- Web Links—these will direct you to helpful Web sites to allow you to conduct further research on quality child care. You will also find links to federal and state organizations and licensing departments.

- Forms—you will find downloadable/printable versions of the forms located in Appendix C of *The ABC's of Quality Child Care*.

- On-line Early Education Survey—this survey gives you the opportunity to respond to what features you like and what features you want to see improved on the Online Resources™.

 The Online Resources™ icon appears at the end of each chapter to prompt you to go on-line and take advantage of the many features provided.

You can find the the Online Resources™ at www.earlychilded. delmar.com

Acknowledgments

I would like to extend a special thanks to my pastor, Dr. Mike Brown; Isela Castanon; Dr. Cristina V. Salas; Alyca E. Stuart Moore; and Minister Lyndon Mayfield. Special appreciation goes to Elvia Walker, Director, and the staff of Logan Child Development Center, Fort Bliss, Texas; and Pat Smith, Child and Youth Services Coordinator, Fort Bliss, Texas.

I also wish to acknowledge a special friend who lives forever in my heart, Cindy Lay. Finally, to all my family and friends who encouraged and supported me to write this book, thank you!

Chapter 1

Starting Out Right

- Quality Care versus Minimum Standards
- Why Is Child Development So Important?
- Developing Your Philosophy: The "Heart" of Your Business

Quality Care versus Minimum Standards

Now that you are opening your own child care facility, or if you have just decided to work with young children, there are many important aspects of child development that you will have to consider.

Today, if you take the time to look around, you will notice quite a few child care settings out there. They vary in size, quality of care, approach to education, and most important, in program development and implementation.

To give you a clear picture of the choices you have, we need to establish the differences between two very distinguished and well-known methods used in caring for children. These methods are custodial and developmental care.

Custodial care is the type of care that only responds to children's basic needs, such as feeding, changing diapers, and keeping the children clean and safe.

On the other hand, developmental care responds to children's basic needs, but has the ultimate goal of helping and supporting children's physical, social, emotional, and cognitive areas of development. It gives young children the love, emotional support, and appropriate care they need to explore and discover the world around them.

Developmental care is supported and implemented by responsive adults in a safe and healthy learning environment for children. Providing quality care is not an easy job, but is by far the most rewarding and provides a real feeling of accomplishment.

Why Is Child Development So Important?

Having a solid understanding of child development is the best and most practical foundation for developing a good program for the children in your care. When we talk about child development, we mean a sequence of physical, intellectual, emotional, and social changes that begin at birth and extend for the entire life of an individual.

Many of the changes that occur in children's lives are a result of experiences they have on a daily basis with adults, peers, and the environment around them. That is why it is so important for child care providers to learn how children grow and develop—so that they can foster daily positive experiences and provide a safe and healthy learning environment.

Understanding how children develop is the most reassuring way of knowing what children should be doing at different stages of development. Having realistic expectations of the children in your care will give you the tools you need to support the children's needs to safely and successfully explore the world around them.

The section that follows provides a developmental outline of different ages and stages of children. The best way to determine if a child is developing well is to have some guidelines as to what children are generally doing at a specific age. Even though this is a brief list, it gives you the basic children's skills you need to be aware of.

Keep in mind, however, that children are unique individuals who develop and master skills at different times. Just because one child starts to walk at 11 months does not mean that all infants have to walk at the same age. If you are concerned about the development of a child, or you are not sure on how to make a child development assessment, you can call a local early childhood intervention care line. Find your state in Appendix B to obtain the contact information for your state's licensing and registration office, which can help you access assessment and intervention services and information.

Children's Development Ages and Stages

Birth to Six Months

- explores the environment through the mouth, eyes, and ears
- looks to see who is talking
- responds to voices and noises
- follows objects
- attempts to reach for objects
- builds coordination to bring objects to the mouth
- reaches for toys or interesting objects placed nearby
- rolls over
- picks up head and chest when lying on the stomach
- makes sounds to get attention
- gurgles and smiles spontaneously
- laughs out loud
- recognizes voices and faces of parents and primary caregivers
- imitates sounds

Six to Twelve Months

- sits without help for a few seconds
- attempts to crawl or creep
- develops coordination of fingers with thumb
- holds small objects
- holds to a toy that is being pulled away
- transfers objects from hand to hand
- drops objects and moves body to find the dropped object
- places everything in the mouth
- begins drinking from a cup
- stands alone briefly
- babbles
- responds to words and names
- imitates and repeats sounds
- recognizes the word *no*
- gets upset when left alone
- plays pat-a-cake and other clapping games
- pulls body up by holding on to a piece of furniture
- walks with help
- pulls and pushes toys around
- attempts to feed self simple finger foods
- experiments with objects by dropping, banging, and throwing them to see what happens
- develops balance
- increased curiosity to explore the world around them

Twelve to Eighteen Months

- stands up alone or walks
- likes to climb
- walks backward
- stoops to pick up objects
- attempts to kick or roll a ball

- stacks a tower of two to three blocks
- scribbles
- pushes/pulls toys
- drops objects into a container and takes them out
- throws ball overhead
- hands over a toy when asked
- able to wave good-bye
- follows simple directions
- increases vocabulary by two to three words besides *mama* and *dada*
- enjoys looking at colorful books
- turns pages of a book
- begins to identify body parts and other objects
- points to a desired object without crying
- helps around the house with simple tasks
- enjoys songs and finger plays
- asks for help
- enjoys playing with other people but is content playing alone
- shows affection to familiar people

Eighteen to Twenty-Four Months
- runs without falling
- kicks a ball without losing balance
- walks backward
- walks up steps
- likes to jump
- attempts to balance on one foot
- moves to music
- sings songs
- uses spoons to eat
- attempts to wash and dry hands

- makes a tower of four to six blocks
- holds large pencils or crayons
- masters scribbling
- pulls off shoes and socks
- undresses self
- strings large beads
- picks up toys and puts them away
- enjoys big and colorful books
- points to pictures and objects when asked to find something
- use words such as *no, more,* and *mine* to express wants
- plays alongside other children
- tests rules and limits
- uses two-word sentences

Two Years Old

- likes to run
- jumps with both feet off the ground
- pedals tricycles
- throws and catches a ball
- jumps over objects
- dresses up self with loose-fitting clothes
- stacks up different sizes of blocks
- assembles construction toys
- turns door handles
- feeds self
- pours milk from a pitcher
- works simple puzzles
- points to and names objects and pictures
- enjoys pretend play (talking on the phone, cooking, etc.)
- understands simple directions such as, "Pick up your toys and put them away"
- enjoys music and instruments
- moves to music
- likes colorful books
- displays rapid increase in vocabulary
- asks questions
- engages in real and imaginary conversations
- displays increased attention span
- copies drawings of circles
- fills and dumps container with water, sand, and different objects
- knows first and last name when asked
- makes two- to three-word sentences
- begins to take turns

Three Years Old

- walks backward
- jumps over objects
- balances and hops on one foot
- builds tall towers with blocks
- builds elaborate block constructions
- cuts paper with scissors
- works puzzles with more and smaller pieces
- string large beads
- enjoys drawing with pencils, markers, and crayons
- participates in group time
- enjoys listening to storybooks
- repeats finger plays and songs from memory
- understands concepts such as: in/out; big/small; over/under
- identifies objects and what they can do
- asks many how and why questions
- likely to be potty trained
- understands and uses plural words
- dresses and undresses self
- brushes teeth
- buttons large buttons
- feeds self with little mess
- washes and dries hands unsupervised
- takes turns
- helps with cleanup times
- understands the concept of sharing
- engages in cooperative play
- enjoys dramatic or pretend play
- loves to play outdoors
- retells stories and relates past events and experiences
- identifies colors, numbers, and letters
- begins to understand and respect the needs of others

Four Years Old

- likes to run, jump, and climb
- walks on balance beams
- able to aim a ball thrown overhand
- bounces a ball
- alternates feet when walking down the stairs
- cuts paper with scissors following a line
- manipulates and makes objects out of play dough
- builds elaborate structures with blocks
- draws simple figures of people with body parts
- knows the alphabet, numbers, and colors
- prints first name
- recalls past events successfully
- counts objects
- identifies strangers
- wants to help with house chores
- asks many questions
- curious about how things work
- follows two or three consecutive directions
- understands rules and limits

- takes care of personal belongings and respects other children's possessions
- knows outside body parts
- likes to sing
- shares ideas and feelings with others
- enjoys listening to storybooks
- uses pictures to read
- identifies letters as symbols of print
- reads a picture book
- engages in conversation using five- to six-word sentences
- enjoys having pretend friends
- likes to explore the entire environment
- acts playfully
- displays a tremendously increased attention span
- listens well
- loves praise and words of encouragement
  Good job, Paul! I like the way you washed your hands before coming to the lunch table.

Five Years Old
- throws and catches balls
- hops on one foot
- ties shoes
- dresses self (zips and buttons clothes)
- rides a tricycle
- cuts with scissors
- feeds self with fork and spoon
- cares for self (combs hair and brushes teeth without help)
- enjoys drawing, cutting, pasting, and painting pictures
- completes more complex puzzles
- shares and takes turns
- separates from parents easily

- knows name and address
- identifies with own ethnic group and sex
- knows body parts
- identifies numbers and letters
- names most shapes and colors
- counts objects and classifies objects into groups
- enjoys singing
- plans own play activities
- enjoys helping around the house
- cares for personal belongings and respects other's possessions

Developing Your Philosophy: The "Heart" of Your Business

One of the most important aspects of running a child care business is to develop your program's philosophy. In other words, philosophy is the foundation of your program. From curriculum to parent communication, everything that you believe and practice in your program should be conveyed to children and their families. Parents need to know about and understand what is taking place in your program and how their children are cared for.

General Aspects to Consider

- The philosophy of your program should be based on the knowledge that children need to be loved and valued for who they are. Their feelings, needs, and interests are respected and always taken into consideration.

- Your program should be noncompetitive. Children are successful and respected because of their accomplishments and the mastering of developmental skills. Their individual capabilities should not be compared with the accomplishments or failures of other children.

- Your program should be nonjudgmental. Accept parents and children for who they are regardless of their race, religion, beliefs, or economical status.

- Your program should take care of business with professionalism and respect for others. Any information regarding families and their children is kept confidential and used only to benefit the children in your care and your program.

- Your program should provide experiences that promote and support children's physical, social, emotional, and cognitive development.

- Your program should offer a variety of developmental interest areas such as:

art	manipulatives	block building
science	music	sand/water play
dramatic play	story time	outside play

- Learning activities implemented in your program should be concrete, real, and relevant for the children.

- Your program should offer opportunities for hands-on experiences, where children can feel and touch the materials.

- Your program should offer multisensory experiences. All activities should foster the use of tactical (touch), auditory (hearing), taste, smell, visual, and motor skills.

- In your program, children should be viewed as whole individuals. All areas of development (cognitive, social, emotional, and physical) should be integrated to provide a balanced and appropriate development of children's skills.

For additional information on quality child care, visit our Web site at **http://www.earlychilded.delmar.com**

Chapter 2

Policies and Registration

Licensing and Registration

Before opening a child care facility, your first step is to register with and/or be licensed by the appropriate local and/or state agencies that regulates child care businesses.

The licensing process is necessary to ensure that all child care businesses at least meet established minimum standards and guidelines for operation. In addition, it ensures that children are properly cared for in a safe and healthy environment. Use Appendix B to find the licensing agency that regulates child care in your state.

Before calling the licensing office make sure you are clear on what your plans are and what your are looking for. During your call, ask the agency representative all the questions you need to help you understand the process of licensing and registration. Do not be afraid or intimidated. The licensing people are there to answer your questions and to help you complete the licensing process.

During the telephone conversation, the licensing person usually will ask about what type of business you plan on starting. With that information, they can help determine what type of licensing you need. There are four basic types of child care licensing available in most states:

1. **Registered family homes.** In registered family homes, caregivers take care of children in their own home. They care for no more than twelve children (counting their own) under age 14.

The maximum number of children allowed in a family home is based on the ages of children and number of staff.

2. **Group day care homes.**   These facilities provide care for less than 24 hours a day for 7 to 12 children less than 14 years of age.

3. **Day care centers.**   Day care centers are any child care facilities of any capacity, other than a family child care home.

4. **Foster homes.**   Households in which a child is raised by someone other than its own parents.

> *Remember: Different states have different types of child care businesses. Contact your local licensing office to find out what is appropriate for your setting. See Appendix B for contact information.*

After establishing what type of licensing you need, the licensing office generally sends out free of charge a complete package with the minimum standards and guidelines and necessary application forms for licensing and/or registration of your business. Once you have received the package, take the time to carefully read all of the material. The more familiar you are with the minimum standards and regulations for your business, the easier it will be to comply with them.

Before starting the application process, most states require you to attend an orientation class given by licensing and regulatory services. The office will let you know the date and place where the meeting is held. In the orientation class, you will review all the necessary application forms and other vital information you need to successfully complete the licensing process. In addition, you can ask questions to clarify any subject that you did not understand about the minimum standards and guidelines and inquire about the application forms.

While getting everything ready to open your doors for business, it is a good idea to have all the necessary policies you need to start and run your child care facility. The sections that follow cover some of the policies and requirements you need to consider.

Number of Children

The number of children that you are allowed to care for will depend on the

- type of the child care licensing you have
- ages of the children
- facility size
- number of staff
- staff's own children

Information on child-staff ratios and grouping can be found in your minimum standards and guidelines package. In it you can find a chart or similar information outlining the different age combinations you are allowed to care for.

Hours of Operation

Like other policies, the hours of operation are important to your business. It is essential that you determine and clearly state your hours of operation to parents. No matter what type of schedule you choose or how many hours the children are in your care, remember to take the parents' needs into consideration.

Here are some common hours used by different child care facilities:

5:30 A.M. .... 6:00 P.M.

6:00 A.M. .... 5:30 P.M.

6:00 A.M. .... 6:00 P.M.

6:00 A.M. .... 6:30 P.M.

7:00 A.M. .... 6:00 P.M.

Do not forget that you can provide extended hours past regular closing time, as well as weekend care if you choose to do so. Before offering extended hours, check with your licensing office or regulating agency for the requirements and any special training you may need.

Enrollment Forms

Enrollment forms contain necessary information about the children in your care and their families. At a minimum, the enrollment forms should contain the following information:

- child's name
- birth date
- home address
- home telephone number
- date of enrollment into the program
- program in which child will be enrolled
- name and address of parents and telephone numbers at which parents can be reached while the child is in care
- name(s) and telephone number(s) of other designated people to contact when parents cannot be reached
- names of people to whom the child may be released
- known food and medication allergies

Different states may require different information about the children and their families. Check the requirements and regulations specific to your state. See Appendix B for contact information for state agencies and organizations that can be of assistance.

Children's Records

Each child in your care should have a file or a record with information that is required by your state's child care regulatory agency. All the information regarding the children in your care and their families must remain confidential and be handled with professionalism. The information acquired should only be used to benefit the children in your care and your program.

To be useful, all children's records must be organized and up-to-date at all times. Records should be available to the facility's personnel

and to state and local child care inspectors, if requested. A child's records should be kept on file at the facility as long as the child is in your care and for at least 12 months after his or her last day. The period each child's file should be kept on record after termination of care varies from state to state.

All children's records should contain the following information:

- enrollment forms
- a written statement from a licensed health professional who has examined the child within the past year
- current immunization records
- name(s), address(es), and telephone number(s) of the child's physician(s)
- a statement of the child's special needs:
    1. known allergies
    2. existing illnesses
    3. previous serious illnesses and injuries
    4. any disabilities and hospitalizations
    5. any medication prescribed for long-term, continuous use
- a record showing that the child has been tested for tuberculosis, if required by your local department of health
- emergency medical treatment authorization
- permission for transportation, if provided
- permission for water activities, if provided
- permission for field trips, if provided
- copies of incident reports
- copies of progress reports, if provided
- copies of receipts for payment, either added to each child's file or kept separately

Filing System

It is important to have the information about the children and their families readily available for inspections and staff's use by maintaining a simple filing system for your business. There are many ways to organize a filing system. A very simple and common way is to keep each child's information in separate folders kept alphabetically in a file cabinet.

Vacations and Holidays

When a child goes on vacation, it is a common practice among child care facilities to charge the parents a fee for holding the child's spot. Some facilities give the parents one or two weeks vacation free of charge per calendar year.

It is a good idea to request that parents provide advanced notice of vacations, allowing you to anticipate and plan for any loss of income during that time. Likewise, you should notify your parents of any vacation or time off that you are planning to take. If you have a small business, and you are going to close it for any period of time, parents will need adequate time to arrange for other means of care for their children. Parents will be particularly grateful if you can offer them a list of backup child care providers and day care facilities that will provide care for the children while you are absent.

Before closing your business on national holidays, you should provide parents with a list of the holidays on which you plan to close. In addition, let parents know about any regular fee they are charged for holidays that fall during your regular operating hours, even though care is not provided.

The most common holidays on which businesses close include:

- Martin Luther King, Jr. Day
- Presidents' Day
- Memorial Day
- Independence Day
- Labor Day
- Columbus Day
- Veterans Day
- Thanksgiving
- Christmas
- New Year's Day

Be aware that some parents may have to work on certain holidays. Many facilities provide care during these holidays for an extra fee, or they assist the parents in arranging substitute care for their children.

Setting Your Fees

The best way to determine how much you should charge for your child care services is to research. Take some time to visit other child care facilities and inquire about their fees and other policies to give you an idea or example of what you need to do.

Experienced child care providers have learned a lot from different situations that helped them set fees or change their policies. They are a rich source of information and they can give you advice on many subjects about your child care business. If you do not know where to go, contact the child care licensing and referral agency for a complete list of child day care homes and day care facilities in your area, or look in the Yellow Pages of the phone book, under Child Care.

Generally, the amount of hours the children spend in your care determines the type of program the parent has to pay for. Here are examples of the programs you may offer:

- **Full-day program.** Children are in your care for 25 hours or more per week.
- **Part-day program.** Children are in your care for more than 10 hours and up to 25 hours per week.
- **Hourly care.** Children are in your care for up to 10 hours per week.

Again, these are regular programs that are available at most child care facilities. Since you are setting up your own policies, you are the one who has to decide what type of programs to offer.

Many other factors are also relevant to setting your fees. Here are some other things to consider.

- **The area in which you live or want to open your business.** An area with a higher cost of living allows for higher fees.

- **Ages of the children in your care.** In most states, the age of the children plays an important role in setting up your fees. Generally, infant care is more time-consuming and consequently more expensive than care for children of other ages. In addition, the adult-child ratio is as low as three to four infants per one adult.

- **Extra activities and services you may offer to meet the needs of the families in your community.** Extra curriculum activities and services enhance your program and the cost can be added to your regular fees. Some ideas of extra activities and services you may offer and charge for include:

    1. water activities

    2. computer classes

    3. music lessons

    4. transportation

- **Various overhead costs, including:**

    1. staff

    2. utilities

    3. janitorial supplies or services

    4. trash removal

    5. insurance

    6. rent or mortgage payment

    7. office supplies and equipment

    8. advertising

    9. children's toys and equipment

 *Don't forget to consider everything, including your overhead, when setting your fees. You want to be affordable, but you also want to make a profit.*

Payment Schedule

There are many different payment schedules used by child care businesses. Some providers have weekly, biweekly, or monthly payment schedules.

A Few Tips

- The best way to avoid any problems with payment schedules is to put your payment policies and schedules in writing for parents to read and sign, before you begin caring for their children.

- It is always a good idea to receive payment in advance. Payments can be made on the first business day of the week or of the month.

- Be flexible on payment schedules and take the parents' needs into consideration.

- Depending on the size of your business, you need to establish a consistent and effective method of receiving and recording payments. The most common ways are receipt books, ledger sheets, and computer software programs, all of which are widely available.

- Make sure you always offer payment receipts to parents and keep copies with your business records.

Late Fees

Because your business will deal with many different families, it is inevitable that you will have problems related to pickup time and payment schedules. The best way to enforce your policies is to notify parents in advance about late fees they may face if they do not comply with the policies you have established.

Here are some examples of late fees.

- Many child care facilities establish a late fee for parents who pick up their children after regular closing time. For example, the parents are charged $3.00 for every 15 minutes after closing time.

- For late payment, a fee of $10.00 might be assessed if payment is not made on time.

Make sure you are flexible and understanding of your parents' problems and needs. From time to time they may have a legitimate reason for not complying with the policies. Remember that not all parents are out to take advantage of you or your business.

Termination Policies

Because this is your business, you have the right to create your own termination policy.

Generally, child care facilities require two weeks' notice from parents if they decide to remove their child from your care. That should help you plan ahead for the loss of income and make that child's slot available to other families. Likewise, you also need to give parents at least two weeks' notice if you decide to stop caring for their child.

If an emergency requires immediate action for child care termination, you need to be patient and consider all possibilities available to help the parents arrange other means of appropriate care for their child. Emergencies that might prompt termination include:

- child consistently hurts him- or herself, teachers, or other children
- child is extremely unhappy and unable to participate and adjust to the program
- parents do not comply with the facility's policies
- parents are not satisfied with child care program

Whatever the case may be, remember to handle terminations with professionalism and respect for others!

Personal Belongings

It is up to you to allow the children to bring personal belongings to your program.

Your program should already be equipped with a variety of appropriate toys available throughout the day for children to enjoy. Additional toys from home can cause conflicts among children that result in fights, losses, and breakage of toys.

If the children want to show off a toy, movie, or a new book, you can set aside one day for show-and-tell. Children will be excited to bring their toys to your program on a special day to share with their friends.

Clothing

Children should arrive clean and dressed in comfortable play clothes that are easily washable and allow freedom of movement.

All clothing should be appropriate for the season or weather. An extra set of clothing should be brought every day or kept at the facility for emergencies.

To avoid mix-ups, it is a good idea to have the clothing labeled with each child's name.

Jewelry

Jewelry is a very attractive item to children, and for some families is an issue of religion and tradition. Make sure you consider parents' needs and the safety of the children, when establishing your policies on jewelry.

Incident Reports

Children are in almost constant motion. They are active learners and explorers and their curiosity leads them to great adventures.

Because children are always up and about, accidents will happen in your program. It is a good idea to have some type of documentation of accidents, as well as the situations that need to be addressed with the parents.

Having written documentation of accidents or other incidents protects your business against false allegations of child abuse or neglect. This is important for your own protection. Remember to give a copy of the incident report to the parents and keep a copy in the child's file.

Some states have specific forms for incident reports. Be sure to check out the requirements for your local area and get copies of any mandated forms. See Appendix B for contact information.

Sample Incident Report

Figure 2–1 shows a sample incident report for a common situation in a child care setting. A blank form is included in Appendix C for your use.

Feedback Sheets

A great idea to keep the parents involved in their child's care is to provide them with feedback sheets. These sheets are usually given to parents of young children and contain information about their child's activities, eating habits, and other types of information that you would like to share.

Most parents love to receive a feedback sheet at the end of the day about their child's activities. Knowing what is taking place in their child's life while they are absent can help them feel more comfortable and secure.

FIGURE 2–1   Sample Incident Report

CHILD'S NAME: _Laura Williams_

ROOM: _Preschool_

DATE: _7/7/02_

TIME: _9:30 A.M._

ACTIVITY PLACE (Place Where the Situation Occurred):

House area

DESCRIPTION OF OCCURRENCE:

Laura was playing in the house area with some dolls. Another child tried to take the dolls away from Laura and scratched her on the right cheek.

NOTIFICATION OF SUPERVISOR:

Yes (X)   No ( )

ACTIONS TAKEN:

I helped Laura say to the other child "scratching hurts." I also washed Laura's right cheek with water and soap as I comforted her with lots of TLC.

SUGGESTED FOLLOW-UP:

None

STAFF SIGNATURE: _Thelma C._

DATE: _7/7/02_ TIME: _2:30 P.M._

PARENT OR GUARDIAN SIGNATURE: _Roger Williams_

DATE: _7/7/02_ TIME: _4:30 P.M._

At the very least, daily feedback sheets should contain information about

- nutrition
- sleeping patterns
- toileting and diapering
- special activities or experiences
- supplies needed
- caregiver's comments or concerns

Sample Feedback Sheet

Figure 2–2 shows a sample feedback sheet for a toddler. A blank feedback sheet is found in Appendix C.

Child's Progress Report

The child progress report is another way to share important information about the children in your care with their parents. This report should contain information such as:

- skills or concepts the child has learned or is working on
- child's good behavior
- child's good thinking

A child progress report is similar in format to an incident report form. The main difference is that the progress report discusses developmental milestones and accomplishments rather than problem situations. Figure 2–3 shows a sample progress report. A blank progress report form is available in Appendix C.

FIGURE 2–2   Sample Feedback Sheet

Daily Feedback Sheet

CHILD'S NAME: *Alex Ramos*

ROOM: *Toddlers*

DATE: *5/9/02*

DIAPER CHANGING: **INITIALS**

Time:	8:00	Asleep	(Dry)	Wet	Loose	Firm	Provider: *AC*
Time:	9:50	Asleep	Dry	(Wet)	Loose	Firm	Provider: *AC*
Time:	12:00	Asleep	Dry	Wet	Loose	(Firm)	Provider: *AC*
Time:	14:00	Asleep	Dry	(Wet)	Loose	Firm	Provider: *AC*
Time:	15:30	Asleep	Dry	(Wet)	Loose	Firm	Provider: *AC*

EATING RECORDS:

Time: 7:30   **Child drank/ate:** *Milk, cereal, and bananas*

Time: 9:00   **Child drank/ate:** *Apple juice, crackers, and cheese*

Time: 11:30   **Child drank/ate:** *Milk, green beans, peaches, rice, and meatloaf*

Time: 14:30   **Child drank/ate:** *Grape juice and blueberry muffins*

SLEEPING RECORDS:

Time: 12:00   To   14:00

Time: To

Time: To

CAREGIVER NOTES OR COMMENTS:

Alex did a good job setting the table for lunch today!

Do not forget to bring Alex's diapers and wipes for next week. Thanks.

FIGURE 2–3   Sample Progress Report

CHILD'S NAME: _Christina Miller_

ROOM: _Toddlers_

DATE: _1/15/02_

TIME: _2:00 P.M._

ACTIVITY PLACE:

Block area

DESCRIPTION OF OCCURRENCE:

Christina was playing with her friends when she suddenly looked at me
and said, "potty."

ACTIONS TAKEN:

I immediately took Christina to the bathroom and helped her sit on the
potty chair. After she was done, we all clapped and praised her for a
job well done!

SUGGESTED FOLLOW-UP:

We are going to encourage Christina to use the potty more often.
Also, we are going to set up a potty conference with her parents.

STAFF SIGNATURE: _Carol Menendez_

DATE: _1/15/02_   TIME: _2:30 P.M._

PARENT OR GUARDIAN SIGNATURE: _Stephanie Moore_

DATE: _1/15/02_   TIME: _5:30 P.M._

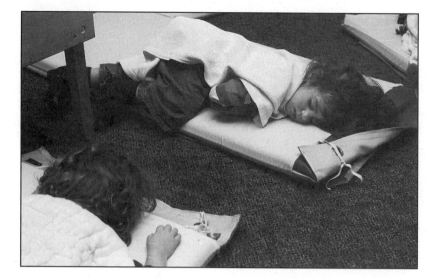

Quiet Time

Rest periods should be provided that are appropriate to the ages and needs of children. At least one hour of rest scheduled for all children up to the age of five.

If the children are not asleep or tired, you should provide quiet activities as an alternative to naps. Table toys, puzzles, or books are excellent ideas for quiet activities that should not disturb other children who are resting.

Remember! Nap time should be encouraged, but not forced on the children.

Meals

All meals served to the children must be nutritious and follow guidelines recommended by USDA Child Care Food Program. Child care providers usually supply breakfast, lunch, and snacks, with the cost included in the program fee. All providers require parents to bring formula, baby food, or any other special dietary foods for their children.

To obtain information on nutrition or food programs for reimbursement of children's meals, you can contact your state agency that handles nutrition programs. In Appendix B, find your state and look

for the agency that lists nutrition programs. That agency will provide you with eligibility requirements, as well as the times, quantities, and types of food to be served.

Birthdays and Other Special Occasions

Child care providers enjoy sharing and participating in the children's special celebrations and birthday parties. However, you need to be careful about the types of foods or treats you will allow your parents to bring to the program. It is advisable to follow your state policies and not allow the parents to bring candy, gum, or any other type of food or treats that are not nutritious and present a choking hazard.

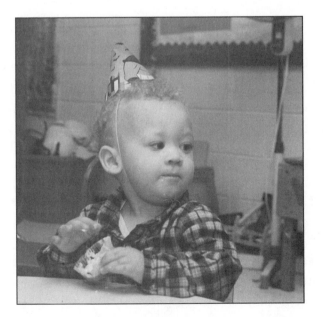

Health and Safety

For health reasons, children that show signs of inadequate hygiene, fever, diarrhea, severe cold, unusual rash, or communicable disease should not be allowed to attend the program with other children.

When children are sick, they usually need more attention and care than you are able to give because you have other children to care for. Sick children need to stay home until they are well and again able to participate in the activities of the program.

If a child presents signs of illness or is injured while in your program, you must handle the situation with caution to protect the health of other children. Isolate the child from the rest of the group and immediately notify the parents to pick up the child. The child may return to the program as soon as the child is well and in good health.

Table 2–1 provides information about some of the most common diseases you may encounter and guidelines for prevention and treatment.

Immunization Records

Each child of your program should have a current immunization record. These records should be kept up to date and maintained as part of your filing system. Each immunization record should include:

- child's birth date
- vaccine type and number of doses
- dates (month/day/year) the child received each immunization
- rubber stamp or signature of the physician or health personnel administering the vaccine

Administering Medication

If any children require medication during their stay in your program, it is very important that you follow your state's requirements for dispensing medication. Most states have minimum requirements that include the following:

- A record must be made of the following and kept for at least three months:
    1. name of the child to whom the medicine was given
    2. name of the medication
    3. date, time, and amount of medication given
    4. name (not initials) of staff administering the medication
- To administer medication to the child, written parental permission is required.
- Follow directions stated on the label or as amended by a physician.
- Any medication brought by parents for their child(ren) must be
    1. in the original container
    2. labeled with the child's name
    3. labeled with the date
    4. include directions to administer the medication
    5. if prescribed, include the name of the prescribing physician
- Medication must be
    1. refrigerated, if refrigeration is required, and kept separate from food
    2. kept out of reach of children or in locked storage
    3. current, based on the expiration date on the label
    4. carefully checked for specific dosage or amount before giving to the child to prevent errors

Parent Handbook

Now that you have established the policies and regulations for the operation of your program, you need a consistent method of recording and sharing all this information.

The purpose of a parent handbook is to share information about the policies, regulations, and goals of your program, and to promote cooperation between parents and staff. By giving parents a solid understanding about your program, long-lasting relationships based on trust and security can be developed.

TABLE 2–1   Common Diseases

CONDITION	INCUBATION	EARLY SIGNS OF ILLNESS
AIDS/HIV Infection	Variable	Weight loss, generalized swelling of the lymph nodes, failure to thrive, chronic diarrhea, tender spleen and liver. Individuals with HIV infection may be asymptomatic.
Chicken Pox	10–21 days	Fever and rash consisting of blisters that may appear first on head, then spread to the body. Usually two or three crops of new blisters that heal leaving scabs.
Common cold	1–3 days	Runny nose, watery eyes, general tired feeling, cough.
Conjunctivitis Bacterial and/or Viral	1–3 days	Red eyes, with some discharge or crust on eyelids.
Fever		Oral temperature 38°C (100.4°F) or greater.
Head Lice (Pediculosis)	Eggs hatch in 7–10 days	Itching and scratching of scalp; pinpoint white eggs.
Hepatitis, Viral Type A	15–20 days avg. 28 days	Abrupt onset of fever, tired feeling, stomachache, nausea, or vomiting followed by jaundice. Young children may have mild case of diarrhea without jaundice.
Hepatitis, Viral Type B	2–6 months	Gradual onset of fever, tired feeling, loss of appetite.
Herpes Simplex (Cold Sores)	First infection 2–12 days	Blisters, on or near lips, that open and become covered with dark crust. Recurrences are common.
Impetigo	Variable, usually 3–7 days	Blisters on skin that open and become covered with yellowish crust; no fever.
Infectious Mononucleosis	30–50 days	Variable. Generally asymptomatic in infants and young children. Symptoms when present include fever, fatigue, swollen lymph nodes, and sore throat.
Influenza	1–3 days	Rapid onset of fever, headache, sore throat, cough, chills, lack of energy, and muscle aches.
Meningitis, Bacterial	2–10 days	Sudden onset of fever, headache, and stiff neck, usually with some vomiting.
Meningitis, Viral	2–10 days	Sudden onset of fever and headache, usually with some vomiting.
Ringworm of the Body	4–10 days	Slowly spreading, flat, scaly, ring-shaped spots on skin. The margins may be reddish and slightly raised.
Tuberculosis, Pulmonary	4–12 days	Gradual onset of tiredness, loss of appetite, slight fever, failure to gain weight, and cough.

NOTE: The major criterion for excluding a child from attendance is the probability of spreading the illness from person to person. A child may have a nonexcludable illness but still require care at home or in a hospital.

EXCLUDE CHILD FROM ATTENDANCE

No, unless a child's physician determines that a severe or chronic skin eruption or lesion that cannot be covered poses a threat to others. The child's parents and physician should be advised in the case of measles, rubella, or chicken pox outbreaks at the child care facility that may pose a health threat to the immunosuppressed child.

Yes

No, unless fever is present (see Fever).

Yes

Yes

Yes

Yes

No

No

Yes

No, unless fever is present (see Fever).

Yes

Yes

No, unless fever is present (see Fever).

No

Yes

NOTES FOR PREVENTION/TREATMENT

Teach importance of hand washing. When cleaning up spills of blood or body fluids, wear gloves and use a suitable disinfectant.

Vaccinate child.

Teaching importance of hand washing and covering mouth when coughing or sneezing.

Teach importance of hand washing. Allergic conjunctivitis is not contagious.

Shampoo or lotion treatment immediately upon discovery. Second shampoo or lotion treatment in 7 to 10 days is recommended. Teach importance of not sharing combs, hats, and coats.

Teach importance of good hand washing. Immune globuline should be given to household contacts. If more than one case occurs in a child care facility immune globulin should be considered for all children and parents involved.

Vaccine available but recommended for high-risk groups only as opposed to the general public. Neither cases nor carriers excluded from attendance. Teach importance of good hygiene and avoid contact with blood/body fluid of recent cases or chronic carriers.

Teach importance of good hygiene. Avoid direct contact with sores.

Keep lesions covered while at the child care facility. Teach importance of hand washing and keeping fingernails clean.

Minimize contact with saliva or nasal discharges. Teach importance of hand washing. No vaccines or specific treatment have been recommended in routine cases.

Vaccine available, but only recommended for children with certain chronic diseases. Antiviral therapy available for cases of influenza type A.

Report suspect cases to local health department or state health department. Depending on which bacteria are causing the illness, prophylactic antibiotics may be recommended for family members. Occasionally, close contacts at a child care facility are also treated.

Teach importance of hand washing. Prophylactic antibiotics of no value.

Treatment is recommended. Keep lesions covered while at the child care facility.

All classroom contacts should have TB skin tests. Antibiotic prophylaxis indicated for newly positive reactors.

Source: Adapted from Texas Department of Health, 25 TAC § 97.6, effective September 1, 1987.

Here are five important tips to remember when developing your parent handbook:

1. The parent handbook must be organized.
2. The parent handbook should contain all policies, regulations, and goals necessary for the operation of your program.
3. The parent handbook should also contain your philosophy for the development and well-being of the children in your care.
4. Your parent handbook must be updated when any changes of policies and regulations occur.
5. Parents should be strongly encouraged to visit your program at any time.

Parent Handbook Contents

There are six areas that should be covered in your parent handbook.

1. **Introduction.** It is a good idea to begin the handbook by stating the basic philosophy of your program. Generally, parents want to know your beliefs about child development and how your program will benefit the lives of their children.
2. **General policies.** Include information about:
   - state licensing
   - registration
   - hours of operation
   - vacations
   - holidays
   - fees
   - payment schedule
   - late fees
   - termination policies
   - personal belongings
   - jewelry
   - clothing
   - birthdays and other special occasions
   - other policies you may want to share

3. **Safety.** Include information about:
- guidance and discipline
- sign-in /-out procedures
- emergency procedures
- accident reports
- fire safety

4. **Health.** Include information about:
- food and nutrition
- mealtimes
- medical requirements
- medications
- illnesses
- toileting
- cleanliness

5. **Parent involvement.** Include information about:
- open houses
- parent volunteer program
- communication
- parent conferences
- newsletters
- bulletin boards
- lesson plans

6. **Other services.** Include applicable information about:
- field trips
- extracurricular activities

Funding Your Business

Today with the increasing number of parents working outside of their homes, quality child care facilities are in great demand.

Taking care of children and providing them with a safe, healthy, and exciting learning environment can cost you a great deal of money. Don't be discouraged! There are many sources of funds available to finance your child care facility. Knowing the right places to go and whom to see can bring you one step closer to turning that perfect business idea into reality.

Here are a few examples of how to raise funds for your business.

- Save all the money you can and set it aside for your business adventure.
- Borrow money from relatives and close friends.
- Sometimes a business partner can bring extra funds into your business.
- Initiate fund-raisers around your community.
- Secure a small business loan.

For more information about how to fund your business, as well as other legal advice, you can contact the U.S. Small Business Administration in your area. There are hundreds of these offices throughout the country that offer free consulting services on just about every aspect of business operations.

The U.S. Small Business Administration does not offer specific information on how to open and run a child care business. However, U.S. Small Business Administration staff can assist you with developing your business plan and securing financial support that is available to you. Take advantage of these free services and put their knowledge to good use! Many of the agencies listed in Appendix A and Appendix B also can provide information about financial support for your program.

Marketing Your Business

The first step to market your business is to identify all the strengths of your business and how you can help your prospective clients.

There are many different and inexpensive ways to advertise. Take the time to research and find out what method is going to work best for you and your business. Some types of inexpensive advertisements include:

- fliers and brochures
- business cards
- classified ads
- referral agencies
- Yellow Pages ads

Whatever method of advertisement you choose, always remember to convey the best information you have to the public. When people know that what you offer is good and recognize they need it, they will most likely come to you for help.

Once again, the U.S. Small Business Administration can help you develop a good marketing plan for your business, so to learn more about advertising and promoting your business, contact your local office. Remember, their services are free of charge and can be of great help to you. Take advantage of them, they are there to help, encourage, and support good business ideas.

This chapter is intended to give you a general idea of policies and regulations that you need to consider in starting a child care business. Please refer to the agencies listed in Appendix B for specific regulations and licensing procedures for starting a child care business in your state.

For additional information on quality child care, visit our Web site at **http://www.earlychilded.delmar.com**

Chapter 3

Safety

- Safety
- Providing Safe Indoor and Outdoor Environments
- Toy Safety Checklist
- Teaching Children Safety Rules
- Emergency Precautions
- Emergency Procedures for Injuries
- Communicable Diseases
- Fire Safety

Safety

Children are active learners. They like to run, jump, explore, and do everything their curiosity and imagination drives them to do. Children need to feel secure and trust their environment to be able to freely explore and take risks on learning experiences. Child care providers are responsible for providing a safe environment by reducing hazards.

Providing Safe Indoor and Outdoor Environments

- Supervise children at all times.
- Keep children within an adult's view from any point of a room or in an outside area.
- Organize indoor and outdoor areas so children can move freely.
- Check indoor and outdoor environments for sharp objects, exposed electrical outlets, and poisons including mouse and roach traps.
- Use safety outlets or electrical outlets must have childproof covers.
- Check materials and equipment for broken parts or jagged edges.
- Replace or repair damaged materials or equipment immediately.
- Have brooms and mops available for cleanups.
- Make sure that all materials and equipment are easy to clean.
- Ensure that all equipment is properly scaled and designed for children's use.

- Keep cleaning products out of children's reach and securely locked away in a cabinet.
- Make sure that all play equipment for children under two years old is large enough to prevent swallowing or choking.
- Do not use concrete, asphalt (hard), and other hazardous surfaces in fall zones. Climbing materials and swings should be on soft surfaces.
- If possible, always provide duplicates of toys to prevent unnecessary struggles.
- Clearly mark glass doors with decals or other materials placed at children's eye level.
- Install all heavy equipment properly with brackets or anchors to prevent tipping over or collapsing.
- Always use low, open shelves for storage.
- Organize shelves with heavier toys on bottom shelves.
- Keep teacher's materials, scissors, staplers, knives, or other dangerous equipment out of children's reach.

Toy Safety Checklist

- Toys are nontoxic.
- Toys are easy-to-clean.
- Toys are nonflammable.
- Toys are nonbreakable.
- Toys are in good condition for easy manipulation by children.
- Toys are appropriate for each different age group.
- Toys with small parts are not available to small children to prevent any choking hazard situations.
- Toys are free of lead paint. Toys with peeling paint are not allowed in the program.

Always check materials and equipment to ensure safe environment free from hazards.

Teaching Children Safety Rules

- Talk to children about being safe and safety rules as often as you can.

- Ask children to help develop safety rules.

- Write the rules down and hang them throughout the classroom at children's eye level. For younger children, pictures can help them identify the rules.

- Make sure that safety rules are clear and simple.

  Keep the water in the water table.

  We sit on chairs and climb on climbers.

  Use your walking feet in the classroom.

  Use your words instead of your hands.

  No pushing. It hurts.

- Explain the rules with simple words and repeat them often.

  This is the bike riding path.

  Books belong on the shelves.

- Be consistent following the rules. If a certain behavior or activity is unacceptable today, make sure it will be unacceptable tomorrow.

- Always acknowledge and praise the children that follow the rules.

  Good job, Paul! I like the way you picked up the toys from the floor.

- Let the children know why it is important to be safe.

  I need to you to keep the water in the water table, so that no one can slip on the wet floor and fall down.

- Be a role model. Children also learn about safety by watching you.

  I am going to pick up these toys from the floor so no one will trip over them and get hurt.

An effective way to provide a safer environment to the children in your care is to take a safety walk throughout your facility. Whenever possible get down on your knees and pretend to be a child for a moment. Your perspective of environment as an adult will be different than a child's view. Take the time to look throughout your entire environment and make all necessary changes to ensure the children's safety.

Children need consistency to know what is expected of them. If the child continually breaks the rules, remove the child from the situation and redirect the child to an acceptable behavior or activity.

Constant supervision and frequent reminders are always necessary for children's protection.

Emergency Precautions

- Make sure all adults caring for the children have current CPR and first aid training.
- Be sure that a guide for first aid emergency care is always accessible to all personnel of the facility.
- Ensure that first aid kits are stocked and available to all personnel of the facility at all times.
- Develop and post emergency procedures.
- Keep an updated file on each child in your care.
- Practice fire and other emergency drills with the children in your care.
- Keep all parents' telephone numbers within easy access or by the telephone.
- Place emergency telephone numbers on or near each telephone of the facility.

Staff should know if there is 911 service in your area. In addition, there are a number of important emergency numbers you need to post.

1. local police or sheriff's department
2. fire department
3. child abuse hotline (see Appendix B)
4. poison control center
5. department of protective and regulatory services
6. city/county health department immunization program
7. numbers at which parents can be reached
8. numbers of children's physicians designated by the parents

Safety Drills

Safety drills should be conducted at least once a month. Children learn what to do and how to react to a real emergency by repeatedly practicing the drills.

An emergency evacuation and relocation plan must be posted on each room of the facility used by the children. In case of an emergency, the facility's first responsibility is to move the children to a designated safe area where they must be supervised at all times.

Another safety drill you should practice with the children in your care is an intruder or stranger drill. The more children know about strangers and what they should do, the more capable the children will be of defending themselves in unfamiliar and dangerous situations.

Emergency Procedures for Injuries

- First, be calm! Take control of the situation.
- Examine the child carefully to determine how injured or ill the child is.
- Act quickly to give the child the proper care.
- Provide first aid treatment or CPR (cardiopulmonary resuscitation), if needed.
- In the case of critical illness or injury, call 911 or your local emergency services.
- Make sure to call the child's physician named by the parents.
- Notify the parents about the situation as soon as possible. If parents cannot be reached, notify the contact person on the emergency list.
- Give the child lots of TLC—tender loving care.
- Fill out any forms or accident reports that need to be completed while the situation is still fresh in your mind.

Communicable Diseases

Minimizing the Spread of Communicable Diseases

- Observe each child in your care for signs of illness on a daily basis.

- Encourage children and adults to wash their hands frequently, especially before handling or preparing food, and after wiping noses, diapering, or using toilets.

- Be sure that sinks are accessible and easy for children to use.

- Always keep soap and disposable paper towels within children's reach. Liquid soap is more sanitary than bar soap.

- Provide facial tissue throughout the facility, and encourage both children and adults to use the tissue when they have to cough or sneeze.

- Regularly clean and sanitize food service utensils, toys, and other items used by children. Discourage the use of stuffed toys, which cannot be sanitized.

- Be sure that diapering and food preparation areas are physically separate from one another. Always keep surfaces in those areas clean, uncluttered, and dry.

- Wash bedding frequently.

- Change children's diapers regularly and immediately after each bowel movement.

- Sanitize changing areas and properly discard soiled diapers.

- Keep changes of clothing on hand and store soiled items in a nonabsorbent container that can be sanitized or discarded after use.

- Discourage children and adults from sharing items such as combs, brushes, jackets, hats, and bedding.

- Sanitize mats and cots on a daily basis.

- Regularly wash dress-up clothes.

- Talk to children about eating right, exercising, and getting enough rest. Reinforce that these are the best ways to stay in good health.

Prevention and Reporting of Communicable Diseases

- Isolate the child who is ill from the rest of children at the facility until she or he can be taken home.

- Determine the state's criteria for excluding and readmitting children with communicable disease in a group care setting.

- Inform all parents of exposed children about the illness. Ask parents to watch their children for signs and symptoms of the disease.

- Observe the appearance and behavior of exposed children and be alert to the presence of disease. Let parents know immediately so that medical advice and treatment can be sought.

- Use sanitizing procedures and encourage staff and children to take extra precautions with hand washing, food handling, dish washing, and general cleanliness.

- Immediately wash, rinse, and sanitize any object or surface that has been soiled with discharge (such as nasal discharge or feces).

- Sanitize all toys that are mouthed and handled by young children on a daily basis.

- Sanitize diaper-changing table, toilets, and potty-chairs after each use.

- If the disease needs to be reported, contact your local county or city health department.

A complete communicable disease chart for schools and child care centers, can be obtained free of charge from your local department of health. See Appendix B for contact information.

Fire Safety

There are 10 basic fire safety precautions that should always be observed.

1. Smoke detectors should be installed throughout the facility.
   - All classrooms need to be equipped with working smoke detectors. They must be installed and maintained according to the manufacturer's instructions and in compliance with requirements of state and local codes.
   - Test smoke detectors every month and replace batteries once a year.

2. Each classroom of the facility must have a working flashlight or other battery-powered lighting in case of electrical failure.

3. The facility must have a fire extinguishing system approved by the fire marshal. This may be a sprinkler system and/or fire extinguishers.

   - Multipurpose (ABC) dry chemical extinguishers work well on wood, grease, flammable liquid, and electrical fires.

   - Every adult in the facility must know where fire extinguishers are located.

   - Every adult in the facility must read the extinguisher's instruction manual to know how to use it properly.

   - Fire extinguishers should be mounted on the wall by a hanger or bracket. They must be ready and available for staff at all times.

   - Fire extinguishers must be inspected monthly, and the date of the inspection recorded. Fire extinguishers must be serviced when required.

4. Make sure fire drills are practiced regularly. Practice the drills from different locations of the facility or home to familiarize the children and staff with possible exits. Children will know what to do in case of a real fire emergency, if they practice fire drills repeatedly.

5. Plan a facility escape route.

   - Draw a floor plan of your house or facility and decide on the best escape routes.

   - The facility must have two exits to the outside located in distant parts of the facility.

   - Post fire escape routes near room exits and near fire extinguishers. Post the plan where people can view it easily.

   - List a primary and a secondary route of escape, with each having a common meeting place. The common meeting place will help you ensure that everyone is accounted for and safe.

   - Children must be able to open the doors easily from the inside of the facility. Never lock any facility doors between rooms while children are present.

   - The facility must not have any blocked door or pathways.

6. Test doors before opening them. If the door is warm, use another escape route.

7. Get out quickly but carefully!

8. Get out and stay out!

   - React immediately! Do not attempt to rescue possessions or pets. Never go back inside of a burning building.

9. Crawl low under smoke.

   - Heat rises carrying smoke with it, so air will be cooler and cleaner near the floor during a fire. If you run into smoke, try another escape route. If you must exit through smoke, crawl on your hands and knees and keep your head 12 to 24 inches above the floor.

10. Stop, drop, and roll!

    - If your clothes catch on fire, do not run. Stop where you are, drop to the ground, cover your face with your hands, and roll over and over to smother the flames.

    - Cool the burns with cold water and call for help.

Make sure you follow your local safety regulations and requirements that applies to the specific type of child care business you have. See Appendix B for contact information for state agencies and organizations that can be of assistance.

For additional information on quality child care, visit our Web site at **http://www.earlychilded.delmar.com**

Chapter 4

Health

- Good Health and Nutrition
- Providing Healthy Indoor and Outdoor Environments
- Helping Children Develop Good Habits
- Hand Washing
- Toothbrushing
- Diaper Time
- Potty Time
- Sanitizing Procedures
- Infant Feeding
- Mealtimes
- Food Choking and Digestive Hazards

Good Health and Nutrition

Like adults, children need to be in good health to fully use their bodies and minds to explore the world around them.

Child care providers have an important role in helping children to develop healthy habits. If we practice and model good health habits, most likely, our children will develop good habits at an early age and continue them throughout their entire life.

Providing Healthy Indoor and Outdoor Environments

- Provide adequate ventilation and lighting in all rooms. Good ventilation is important to prevent the incubation of germs.
- Open windows daily to let in fresh air.
- Provide comfortable room temperature.
- Provide daily outdoor activities for exercise and fresh air.
- Provide good sanitation throughout your facility.
- Make sure bathrooms are cleaned and sanitized often.
- Be sure that cleaning materials such as bleach solution, brooms, mops, etc., are readily available.
- Sanitize toys and equipment with bleach solution on a daily basis.
- Provide hygiene materials such as paper towels, liquid soap, and toilet paper in places where children can reach.
- Be sure that extra changes of clothes are brought in daily or kept at the facility to be used in case of an emergency.
- Encourage children to pick up and clean up after themselves.

Helping Children Develop Good Habits

- Talk to children about ways to stay healthy.
- Reinforce that eating right, exercising, and getting enough rest are the best ways to stay healthy.
- Be a role model. Model good health practices such as washing hands, eating nutritious food, and brushing your teeth.
- Provide opportunities for children to master self-help skills.

- Allow for children's independence but be there to assist when your help is needed.
- Give the children many praises for practicing good habits.

  Good job, Victoria! I like when you wash your hands after going to the bathroom.

- Show children by words and actions what you are doing and why.

  Paul, I am sweeping the sand off the floor, so that no one will slip and fall.

- Develop health rules. Be simple, clear, and consistent.

  Tara, I need you to go wash your hands before you come to the play dough table.

Hand Washing

Proper hand washing procedures are the most highly recommended way to reduce the incidence of illness and to stop the spreading of germs.

Hand Washing Procedures

- Turn on the water.
- Wet hands and apply the soap. Remember that liquid soaps from a dispenser are more sanitary than bar soaps.
- Rub back of hands and wrists vigorously.
- Scrub both hands together.
- Wash between fingers and under fingernails.
- Rinse hands well.
- While leaving the water running, dry your hands with disposable paper.
- Turn off the water using the paper towel instead of bare hands.
- Properly dispose the paper towel.

An excellent way to teach children hand washing procedures is to display pictures showing the hand washing steps near the sink.

Always model good hand washing procedures and remind your children that washing their hands correctly will help keep them from getting sick.

Times When Adults Should Wash Their Hands

- When arriving at work in the morning
- Before eating or drinking
- Before preparing or serving food
- After using the bathroom
- After assisting a child in the bathroom
- After diapering a child
- After cleaning up messes
- After touching a child who may be sick
- After smoking
- After touching pets

Times When Children Should Wash Their Hands

- When arriving at the child care facility in the morning
- Before eating or drinking
- After going to the bathroom
- After touching a sick child

- Before and after participating in sensory activities such as the water table and play dough
- After coming in from outdoor play
- After touching pets

Toothbrushing

Toothbrushing can be fun for children. Besides teaching them good hygiene, you are helping them to learn basic skills and good habits they will need for the rest of their lives. Here are a few good tips to help teach good dental hygiene.

- Do not offer toothbrushing as a choice. Children need to understand that toothbrushing is a necessity and not a choice. If you want to give them choices, you can offer a choice of two different toothpastes!
- Make sure you model and show children all the right steps for toothbrushing.
- Talk to children about the importance of brushing their teeth correctly.
- Make toothbrushing fun for your children! While brushing, you can make silly faces with the children.

Toothbrushing Procedures

1. Make sure children have their own toothbrush that is labeled with their name.
2. Turn the water on so children can wash their hands.
3. Give children the toothbrush and allow them to wet it.
4. Place a small amount of toothpaste on their toothbrush.
5. Show children how to brush their teeth.
6. Give them a paper or plastic cup. Let them fill the cup with water.
7. Encourage children to rinse their mouth.
8. Let children rinse their own toothbrush.
9. Return toothbrush to proper place to be stored.
10. Encourage children to wipe off their mouth with a paper towel.
11. Praise the children for a job well done!

Children's toothbrushes must be covered and allowed to air dry. They must be kept separate and not touch other children's toothbrushes.

Always remember to check your local licensing regulations to make sure that toothbrushing is permitted. See Appendix B for contact information for state agencies and organizations that can be of assistance.

Diaper Time

Diaper changing should not be just one more responsibility for care providers. It should be an opportunity for care providers and younger children to spend some quality time together in a closer relationship.

Care providers can take advantage of this time to talk, listen, and play with small children in a positive way. It is also important that care providers use appropriate words and positive actions to allow children to feel loved and respected during diaper changing time.

Here are some tips for diaper changing time:

- Talk to children to let them know what you are doing.

  Trey, I am going to clean your bottom with some wipes. It might feel a little cold.

- Hang a mobile over the changing table for children to look at while you are changing their diaper.

- Talk to children during diaper changing about familiar things or sing favorite songs.

- Let children know that diaper changing is a necessity and not a choice.

  I know you don't like to stop playing to get your diaper changed, Maria. I will give you a few more minutes to play and then I will change your diaper.

- Ask the children to help you with small tasks.

  Do you want to hold the diaper for me?

- Help children to feel loved, comfortable, and accepted when changing their diapers.

- Avoid using words to describe diapers that can hurt children such as *stinky* or *messy*.

- Place all supplies for diaper changing within arm's reach of the changing table.

- Provide trashcans for soiled diapers. Trashcans must have lids and be lined with plastic bags. Locking devices for trashcans are also recommended. Trashcans must be emptied as needed during the day.

- Gloves can be very handy and sanitary for changing diapers with bowel movements.
- Make sure bleach solution or a germicidal spray is available to sanitize changing table after each use.
- Antibacterial liquid soap and paper towels should be provided for hand washing.

> *Children should never be left unattended on the changing table for any reason. If you need to leave the changing table, take the infant with you or place the child safely on the floor. Another good idea is to ask somebody to finish changing the diaper for you.*

Diaper Changing Procedures

1. Make sure the changing table is sanitized.
2. Place the child on changing table.
3. Remove the child's clothes.
4. Remove the soiled diaper.
5. Wipe off the child from front to back with wipes or disposable cloths.
6. Place used disposable diaper and wipes in the trashcan.
   - Some state's regulations require that diapers be disposed in plastic bags before being placed in the trashcan.
7. Put a clean diaper on the child.
8. Put the child's clothes back on.
9. Wash your and the child's hands.
10. Place the child in a safe place or direct the child to an activity.
11. Sanitize the changing table.
12. Fill out diaper sheet if provided.

Potty Time

Incorporating Toilet Training in Child Care Facilities

Toilet training is a common request from parents who have their children in child care. Care providers should be willing to assist children in achieving this important milestone.

Toilet training should be a smooth experience for young children. Make sure you recognize the signs that indicate a child's readiness for potty training. There is no right time to start potty training. The time is right when the child is ready. The child needs to be emotionally ready to know what is happening and what is being expected of him. He needs to be physically developed to control the sphincter muscles; in other words, the child needs to be able to hold on and to let go.

When parents and care providers have recognized the child's readiness for toilet teaching, a meeting or potty conference should take place. Discussing potty training policies and strategies will establish consistency between home and school, helping the child master potty training with success.

Helpful Tips

- Consistency must be provided at home and school, and both parties should work as a team.
- Parents should provide complete sets of easy access clothing on a daily basis. Overalls, belts, and tights make it very difficult for children to assist themselves.
- A period should be established to monitor the child's progress. If the child has not been successful during this period, the child might not be ready and toilet teaching should be discontinued for a while. Toilet training can start again when the child shows signs of readiness.
- Parents or any other adult should not establish the right time for toilet teaching.
- Parents and child care providers should demonstrate patience, love, and understanding as they support children developing potty training skills.
- Potty training can be fun and should definitely be a positive developmental experience for young children.

- Most of the time, problems occur because children are not ready for potty training and adults try to do the job for them. The lack of readiness will cause the child to be frustrated and go through unsuccessful and negative experiences that will only delay this wonderful accomplishment.
- Be careful not to show anxiety and frustration to the child.
- Encourage attempts and support all achievements.

Potty Teaching Procedures

1. Take the child to the bathroom and teach her to pull down her clothes.
2. Help the child to sit properly on the toilet or potty-chair.
3. Show the child how to clean up with toilet paper—from front to back.
4. Make sure you give the child a few minutes to try these tasks.
5. Always check the child's bottom for needed assistance.
6. Help the child in getting clothes back up. Remember to let children practice self-help skills as much as possible.
7. Direct the child to the sink and assist her to wash hands; make sure proper hand washing procedures are used.
8. Disinfect toilet seat or potty-chair with bleach solution or a germicidal solution.
9. Wash your hands properly before doing anything else!
10. Fill out diaper sheet, if provided.
11. Always praise children for their efforts! When children are recognized for their accomplishments, they feel good about themselves and they will most likely repeat the behavior or action over and over again.

Sanitizing Procedures

Toys and equipment that are handled or mouthed by children must be sanitized every day.

1. Wash the surface with soap and water.
2. Submerge the toys in a bleach solution.
3. Rinse in clean water and air dry.

Bleach Solution

- Make an effective bleach solution by combining bleach and water in the following amounts:

  1/4 to 1/2 cup of bleach per gallon water.

  1 tablespoon of bleach per quart of water.

- Make and use fresh bleach solution daily. You can stamp or use a china marker to date the spray bottle to ensure fresh solution is being used every day.

- Check your local minimum standards and guidelines handbook for disinfecting with bleach solutions.

- Spray bottles are easy to use and carry around.

CAUTION *Always keep bleach solution and other cleaning supplies out of children's reach!*

Infant Feeding

Feeding times for infants are very special moments. They provide important opportunities for adults to interact with infants in close and caring ways. By looking, talking, playing, and rocking the infant, adults can establish a positive and lasting relationship in which the infant can feel secure and develop a sense of trust.

Infant Feeding Procedures

1. Feed infants according to their individual schedules.
2. Wash your hands.
3. Prepare the bottle.

    - Use bottles that are clean and properly sanitized.
    - Carefully read the instructions on the back of the formula can on how to mix the formula.
    - Formula should be served at room temperature.
    - Always check the temperature of the formula before giving it to the infant.

Most states require the parents to bring the bottles already prepared at home. The bottles are labeled with the child's name, content of bottle, and the date the bottle was prepared. Check your local licensing requirements for bottle-feeding. See Appendix B for contact information for state agencies and organizations that can be of assistance.

4. Place a bib on the infant.

5. Hold the infant in your arms with his head slightly elevated and hold the bottle at the appropriate angle.

   - Always hold the infant during feeding time. Choking, tooth decay, and ear infections are more common among babies who lie down to drink a bottle.

6. Stop periodically to burp the infant. Be sure to have an additional diaper cloth in case he spits up.

7. Take advantage of feeding time to communicate with the infant and show that you care!

8. After the infant is finished, hold him to sleep or place the infant in a safe place for playtime.

Bottles should never be propped or carried by a walking child.

Mealtimes

Mealtime should be a pleasant and enjoyable learning experience for children and adults. It is a time to socialize, as well as learn about good nutrition and eating habits.

 It is not easy for children to learn how to feed and serve themselves. Sometimes it can be very messy! You will have lots of spills and food everywhere. Be patient! Children need many opportunities to practice. It might take some time, but with hard work and your assistance, they will be able to master these difficult skills with success.

There are many ways adults can encourage, assist, and facilitate mealtimes for children:

- Make sure you have everything you will need for mealtimes nearby to avoid making children wait for long periods.
- Proper child-friendly equipment is needed for successful experiences.

- Food should be served in small bowls to allow children to pass the food around the table.
- Model the use of good manners.

  Rachael, please pass me the rice. Thank you, Rachael!
- Encourage the proper use of forks and spoons.
- Allow children to serve themselves!
- Take advantage of this time for language development by talking about things that are relevant for children:

  Children's families

  Things that happened during that day in the program (activities, field trips, special events, etc.)

  The food that they are eating (colors, texture, taste, etc.)
- Set simple and clear rules that can help mealtimes go smoother and turn them into pleasant learning experiences:

  Children need to be sitting properly on their chairs.

  Children should keep their hands to themselves and out of other children's plates.

  Children should be encouraged to eat but not forced.

  Children should be encouraged to clean up after themselves. Be there if help is needed!
- Make toothbrushing a daily routine after mealtimes, if local regulations permit.

Procedures to Make Mealtimes Easier

1. Prepare your children for mealtimes. A quiet activity before mealtimes such as circle time and books will help establish a calm atmosphere.

2. You can also provide soothing, relaxing music in the background before and during mealtimes. Soft instrumental music will do the trick.

3. Make sure you provide proper child-friendly equipment for successful experiences.

4. Encourage children to try new foods. Avoid making a big fuss over food dislikes.

5. Talk about the food being served and role model a positive attitude toward it.

6. Encourage children to help during mealtimes. When children are busy doing constructive work, they are directing their energy toward a positive behavior and they feel good about themselves. Children can assist with:

   • Setting the table

   • Helping friends clean up spills

   • Passing out napkins

   • Cleaning up the tables after mealtimes

7. After children are finished, give them two choices of what to do, while you finish cleaning up the room.

   Ruben, you can get a book to read or play with the puppets, while we get ready for nap time.

   • Make sure the choices you offer are acceptable and can be turned into a daily routine. Children feel secure when they know what to do and that will help you have more control of the classroom during a busy time!

8. Organize yourself! Take the time to observe the children and the environment to find out what is and is not working. It will take more than just a few times to provide pleasant mealtime experiences. Children need to feel a sense of structure in order to make sense of the world around them.

Mealtimes are excellent opportunities to introduce multi-cultural dishes, representing the different backgrounds of your children.

Food Choking and Digestive Hazards

The following list of foods are not recommended for children under two years of age. These foods present a choking hazard and young children may not be able to digest them properly.

- bacon rind
- celery sticks
- corn
- cucumbers
- hard candy
- nuts and seeds
- peanut butter

- raisins and dried fruit
- raw onions
- baked beans
- chocolate
- corn and potato chips

- grapes
- leafy vegetables
- olives
- popcorn
- raw carrot sticks
- honey
- hot dogs

Remember, food for young children should be bite size, and the children must always be supervised during mealtimes. Figure 4–1 provides a sample weekly food menu.

FIGURE 4–1   Sample Food Menu

MONDAY

Breakfast: Milk, bananas, cereal

Snack: Milk, blueberry muffins

Lunch: Milk, meatloaf, green beans, peaches, wheat bread

Snack: Apple juice, crackers

Tuesday

Breakfast: Milk, apricots, French toast w/ syrup

Snack: Cheese cubes, apple slices

Lunch: Milk, baked chicken, broccoli, pineapple, rice

Snack: Trail mix, grape juice

Wednesday

Breakfast: Milk, peaches, oatmeal

Snack: Graham crackers and cheese slices

Lunch: Milk, spaghetti w/ meat sauce, green salad, oranges

Snack: Applesauce, gingerbread

Thursday

Breakfast: Milk, oranges, English muffin w/ jelly

Snack: Fruit salad, yogurt

Lunch: Milk, fish, pears, oven French fries, rolls

Snack: Milk, banana bread

Friday

Breakfast: Milk, fruit cocktail, biscuits w/ jelly

Snack: Grape juice, oatmeal cookies

Lunch: Milk, macaroni & cheese w/ ham, peaches, coleslaw

Snack: Pineapple juice, bread sticks with pizza sauce

Infant's Substitutions

Apple slices—Applesauce	Trail mix—Dry cereal	Orange—Pears, bananas
Broccoli—Green beans	Meat sauce—Browned ground beef	Fruit cocktail—No grapes
Pineapple—Peaches	Green salad—Creamed corn	Coleslaw—Cooked carrots

 For additional information on quality child care, visit our Web site at **http://www.earlychilded.delmar.com**

Chapter 5

Schedules and Routines

- What Is a Good Daily Schedule?
- Why Schedule?
- Routines
- Transition Times

A daily schedule details each day's events and activities that take place in your program. Child care providers must plan and implement a daily schedule that is appropriate and meets the children's needs and interests. Figure 5–1 shows a sample daily schedule.

Schedules are the best way to organize your day. Working with children can be very stressful, but with organization and good planning, things will be much easier for you and your children. Do not be discouraged! Many adjustments and modifications on your daily schedule will be necessary to develop the schedule that will fit the needs of your children and your program.

FIGURE 5–1   Sample Daily Schedule

6:00–7:00	Welcome/free play (books, table toys, etc.)
7:00–8:00	Breakfast
8:00–8:15	Cleanup time
8:15–8:30	Group time (books, stories, songs, finger plays)
8:30–9:30	Free play/art/and other activities
9:30–9:45	Cleanup time
9:45–10:00	Morning snack
10:00–11:00	Outside play
11:00–11:30	Group time or quiet activities
11:30–12:15	Lunch
12:15–12:30	Cleanup/toothbrushing
12:30–2:00	Nap time/quiet activities
2:00–2:45	Free play/small-group activities
2:45–3:00	Cleanup time
3:00–3:30	Afternoon snack
3:30–4:30	Indoor/outdoor play
4:30–5:00	Group time
5:00–5:30	Cleanup time
5:30–6:00	Getting ready to go home

What Is a Good Daily Schedule?

1. Daily schedules should be consistent but flexible enough to meet the needs of the children. For example:

   Going on a field trip to the library to check out the arrivals of new books.

   If a child is engaged in an activity or working hard in a particular project, extend playtime to give the child the opportunity to finish her play. Sometimes a change in the schedule will be necessary to maximize the children's benefits from play.

2. Daily schedules should provide a balance of active and quiet activities throughout the day.

3. Daily schedules should foster opportunities for free choice activities. Children should be able to:

   - Initiate and engage in their own play
   - Participate in small group activities that are set up and offered to them
   - Participate in large group activities
   - Participate in teacher-directed activities (activities that are offered and supervised by an adult)

4. Daily schedules should provide an appropriate amount of time for activities. Children should not be rushed to complete an activity or become bored with the same activity for long periods.

5. Daily schedules for infants should be based on the infant's individual needs. Child care providers must carefully observe infants to learn about their individual eating patterns and other developmental needs.

Why Schedule?

Schedules are used to do a number of things.

1. Organize your day. A good daily schedule will help the day go smoothly, and be enjoyable and less stressful for you and your children.

2. Establish an order of events. For example:
   - Before sitting down at the table for lunch, we need to wash our hands.
   - After playing outside, we sit down in group time to play games that help children relax.

3. Show how long each activity should last. But remember to be flexible! Children should not be rushed to finish any type of activity.

4. Help children learn predictability. Knowing what comes next helps children to trust their environment and feel secure to explore and learn.

5. Help children make sense of their world by watching what is going on around them.

6. Help children develop sense of time.

   A few more minutes to play before we have to pick up our toys.

   This is the way we brush our teeth, so early in the morning.

7. Help children know what is expected of them. Children will not be overwhelmed with activity changes because they know what to do and the choices that are available to them.

Routines

Routines are daily activities and events that happen throughout your day. There are a number of ways to make routines pleasant for both children and adults.

1. Make sure you allow adequate time for routines to be accomplished.
2. Handle routines in a calm and organized environment.
3. Remember to offer as many opportunities as you can for children to be independent, but be there to help if they need your assistance.
4. Ensure that routines are always fun and enjoyable to everyone.

Here are some routines to incorporate into your daily schedule:

- arrival and departure
- toileting/diapering
- hand washing
- eating times
- toothbrushing
- sleeping and resting
- dressing and undressing for outdoors and special activities
- cleanup times

Routines are great opportunities for learning experiences, and can be fun and exciting for everyone. Remember to allow adequate time to accomplish routines and to make sure that children are learning and mastering new skills every day!

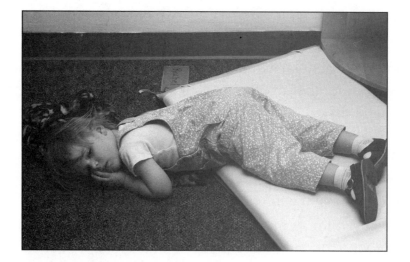

Transition Times

Transition times are important because they help your program move from one activity to another without overwhelming the children with changes in the schedule. Transition times help children to know what is going to take place next. When children know what to do, they feel secure and comfortable with what is going on around them. Transition times also help children to listen, relax, and have positive behaviors and attitudes toward changes.

- Transition times are great opportunities for incidental learning and mastering concepts and skills.
- Transition times are used to avoid disruption of children's play and activities.
- Transition times are planned to avoid making children wait for long periods between activities.

Procedures for Successful Transition Times

1. Before transition times start, give children notice of what is going to take place next:

   A few more minutes to ride your bikes, before we put them away.

2. Help children feel responsible by assigning them tasks:

   A few children will help set up the table for lunch while others will put the books back and toys on the shelves.

3. Allow sufficient time for tasks to be accomplished during transition times.

4. Be clear about giving directions to children during transition times:

   Please park your bikes in the parking area next to the big yellow trucks.

5. Practice transition times every day. Children need lots of repetition to do things on their own.

6. Be creative! Transition times must be fun and relevant to the children's needs. Songs, games, and stories are excellent ideas to incorporate into your transition times.

For additional information on quality child care, visit our Web site at **http://www.earlychilded.delmar.com**

Chapter 6

Physical Environment

- Physical Environment
- Goals and Objectives
- Organizing Your Environment
- Setting up Your Environment with Learning Centers

Physical Environment

The physical environment has a special importance in the development of young children. As we know, children learn by having positive interactions with adults, other children, and with their physical surroundings.

It is very important that care providers take the time to set up their physical environment, both indoor and outdoor spaces. The colors, size of the rooms, furniture arrangement, and other environment aspects have a great influence on children's ability to adapt to the environment.

Goals and Objectives

1. To provide an environment that is free of dangers. Children need to feel secure and safe to freely explore their world and take risks on learning experiences.

2. To provide warmth and a welcoming atmosphere to the children in your care.

    - The room has soft color on the walls.
    - Areas are well lit and there is good ventilation in the room.
    - Furniture is clean, well maintained, and used to define specific play areas.
    - Objects such as plants, soft pillows, rocking chairs, and family pictures are displayed throughout the room.

3. To provide a sense of belonging for children and their families.

    - Children's artwork is attractively displayed at children's eye level.
    - There is a special place for all children to keep their personal belongings, with their name and picture displayed.
    - Pictures with people of different ethnic backgrounds are attractively displayed in the room.

4. To provide a pleasant, organized, and exciting environment for the children.

   • The room is clean, uncluttered, and attractive to children's needs and interests.

   • Low shelves are used to display interesting toys and equipment within the children's reach.

   • A variety of materials and equipment are available for children to explore and learn.

   • Decorative materials such as plants, fish tanks, pictures on the walls, and soft pets (if licensing permits) are present in the room for children to enjoy.

5. To provide a variety of age-appropriate materials, supplies, and equipment that meets children's needs and interests.

   • Toys and equipment are selected to meet the different developmental stages of the children.

   • Toys and equipment support and enhance children's learning experiences and exploration.

   • Toys and equipment are in good condition and sized for children to manipulate.

6. To help children develop relationships with their peers and experience positive interactions with the environment.

- The environment provides opportunities for socialization and allows the children to initiate their own play.
- Play areas are well defined and set up for individual or small-group play.
- The environment is a safe place to explore and learn.

7. To allow for freedom of expression and choices of activities.

- Children are encouraged to initiate their own play and choose between the different appropriate activities offered.

8. To promote children's independence and autonomy.

- Use child-sized furniture throughout the rooms.
- Toys are displayed and organized on low shelves so that children can choose and obtain them without assistance.
- Picture labels are placed on shelves and containers to help children know where each toy or object belongs, making cleanup times easier.
- Toys and equipment that belong to a specific play area are stored together for easy access (e.g., crayons, markers, paper, stamps, and stamp pads belong together in the art area).
- Display charts with pictures at the children's eye level to show children how they can help keep the room clean and organized.

Organizing Your Environment

Having an organized, well-equipped, and an inviting indoor/outdoor environment is essential for learning. When the environment gives children the assurance that "this is a happy and safe place to be," children feel comfortable to explore and discover the wonders of their surroundings.

Setting up Your Environment with Learning Centers

Why Have Learning Centers?

Learning centers allow for small-group activities, which are a good technique to use to work on skills and concepts with the children. Learning centers provide children with hands-on experiences—concrete experiences that children can participate in and learn from directly by doing. Learning centers also foster socialization through interaction with adults and peers.

- When children are involved in appropriate activities offered in the learning areas, their efforts and energy are used to explore and learn.

- Children can manipulate and explore the materials and equipment offered in each learning center to enhance their learning experiences.

- Children can freely choose their own activities and conduct their own play, using the materials provided.

- As children grow and develop, they learn simple rules that are necessary to develop positive relationships with their peers:

    taking turns

    cooperative play

    sharing

    helping a friend

Establishing Learning Centers

When designing a learning center, consider the following:

1. The size of the area will determine the number of children who will be able to work comfortably. Having too many children in one area at the same time may cause confusion and unnecessary disputes.

2. Noise levels—Learning centers that generate similar noise levels should be close to each other, for example:
   - Block area and dramatic play
   - Books and table toys

3. Traffic patterns—Set clear and safe traffic patterns away from children's working areas so children do not have to be constantly interrupted during their activities.

4. Location—Messy and busy areas (e.g., science and sensory and art areas) should be placed near sinks and with uncarpeted floor surfaces.

5. Learning centers must be well defined to eliminate outside distractions and to create manageable environments.

6. Setting clear rules concerning learning centers will help the children feel independent and responsible.

   Selina, when you have a marker in your hands you need to draw on the paper.

   Mark, keep the water in the water table. We do not want our friends to slip on the wet floor and get hurt.

   Kumiko, you need to pick up your table toys before going to the art center.

7. Learning centers should contain a variety of floor surfaces, for example

   - Climbers should be placed on soft surfaces.
   - Use a flat carpet for a hard surface in the block area.
   - Art area should have tile or vinyl floor surfaces for easy cleanups.

8. An adult must be able to see all children from any point of the room at all times.

9. Constantly rotate toys so there is always something new to interest children.

   - To keep your learning centers always interesting for children, you can rotate toys with other activity areas or other child care providers you know.
   - Another great idea to rotate toys is to put some toys away in the closet for a few weeks and bring out some others toys that have been in storage for the children to enjoy. Repeat the same procedure every few weeks. The same toys that the children have played with before will catch their attention and curiosity all over again. It works!

10. Materials and equipment should be accessible to children at all times.

11. Materials and equipment should be organized and well displayed, so children can see what choices are available to them.

12. Shelves should be stocked but not cluttered.

13. Low shelves and furniture are used to divide and define activity areas.

14. Labeling shelves and containers with pictures of the toys helps children identify where the toys go.

15. A developmental environment should contain these specific areas:

- block area
- manipulative area or table toys area
- dramatic play
- music and movement
- quiet area
- library or book area
- science area
- sand and water play
- art center
- wood work
- outdoor play

Remember, if you are limited on space, you can always rotate learning centers. The key point is to set up your environment based on the children's interests.

Setting up the environment is not an easy task. It might take you some time to establish a safe, healthy, and creative environment for your children. The best way to conquer this challenging task is to observe the children using the entire environment. By observation, you can determine the "glows and grows" of your environment that can help foster positive interactions and promote successful learning experiences.

For additional information on quality child care, visit our Web site at **http://www.earlychilded.delmar.com**

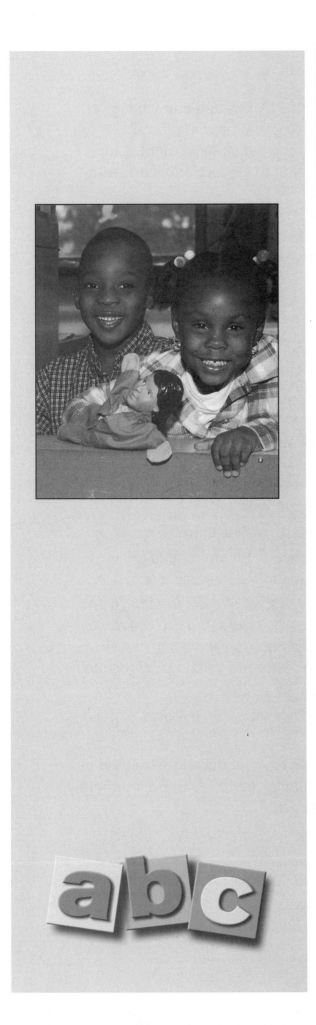

Chapter 7

Activity Areas

- Group Time
- Musical Activities
- Art Center
- Manipulative Area
- Sensory Experiences
- Science Area
- Dramatic Play
- Block Area
- Library or Book Area
- Outdoor Activities
- Quiet Area: A Place to Escape

Group Time

Group time should be a time for fun activities and enjoyment for everyone. You can take advantage of group time to promote socialization, language development, creative movement, and anything else that encourages children to explore and learn with confidence and success.

Group time is a time to talk. Talk to children about familiar things, daily activities, and experiences such as:

- nature changes
- families
- favorite activities, food, songs, and books
- friends, feelings, and fears
- celebrations (birthdays, new siblings, potty training success)

There are a number of ways to provide fun and appropriate group time.

1. Allow the children to participate and talk.
   - Ask the children to retell a story they know.
   - Help children recall past events. Children need to understand how past events relate to present time.

     Yesterday, when we did not pick up the toys from the block area, our friend tripped over the blocks and fell. Today after we finish playing in the block area, we are going to pick up all the blocks from the floor. That way nobody will get hurt.

2. Extend children's play by asking questions:

   John, great answer! Frogs do live in a pond. What else do you think lives in a pond?

3. Ask open-ended questions. These types of questions allow the children to answer with more than a simple yes or no, promoting creativity and language development.

   Halle, what do you think will happen when you mix the green and yellow colors?

   How do you feel when you get hurt?

   Ramon, how did you put these blocks together?

4. Help children express their feeling and ideas by giving them words:

   Sarah: *Me tired.*

   Teacher: *I know you are tired, Sarah. Would you like to take your nap now?*

5. Listen attentively to what children have to say. Listening is a good way of promoting communication by respecting children's opinions, ideas, and feelings.

6. Provide group time activities that encourages children to use all their senses to explore and learn. For example, the goals for a group nature walk include:

   - Children will be able to see the various elements of nature (sun, clouds, sky, birds, etc.).
   - Children will be able to hear the birds, leaves on the trees, the wind, etc.
   - Children will be able to touch the sand, rocks, leaves, and bugs to experience texture, shape, color, and smell.

7. Provide group activities that will encourage children to talk to each other.

8. Make time for songs and finger plays.

   - Plan to introduce at least one new song or finger play each week.
   - Sing familiar songs and finger plays every day.
   - Let children choose the songs they want to sing. Sometimes children will sing the same songs over and over again. Be patient!
   - You can enhance children's songs by offering instruments, clapping hands, or just moving to the music.

9. Be motivated and participate in children's play.

10. Tell stories and read books.

    - Plan at least one story time each day.
    - You can use different materials to enhance and keep the children interested in story time:

flannelboard	tapes
puppets	special guests
books	videos
pictures from magazines	

- For older infants and toddlers, big and colorful books with just a few words will grab their attention more easily.
- When reading or telling children a story, remember to allow time for children to participate and give you feedback.

Remember to read books and tell stories that are appropriate for the age group of the children you are working with.

Tips for Making Group Times Easier

When planning group times, make sure you take into consideration the age group of children you are working with. Younger children have shorter attention spans. Keep group times for this age group short or for as long as the children's interest is maintained.

- Group time for children must be fun and exciting. Whatever activity you decide to do during group time, it needs to promote excitement and interest.
- It is also a good idea to have other activities available along with group time, giving the children the freedom to choose between activities.

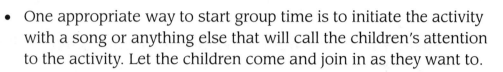

- One appropriate way to start group time is to initiate the activity with a song or anything else that will call the children's attention to the activity. Let the children come and join in as they want to.

- If you are working by yourself, make sure the other activities you offer along with group time do not require close adult supervision, so you can be engaged in the group activity without having to completely divide your attention.

- Group time can be an excellent activity for transition times. Reading a favorite book or just taking the time to relax can set the stage for the next routine or activity.

- All the materials and equipment used in group times should be age appropriate.

- Be flexible! Plan your group time activities according to the children's developmental needs and interests.

- Plan a balanced schedule between indoor group time activities and outdoor group time activities.

Musical Activities

Musical activities are fun and children always enjoy participating!

1. Music should be part of our daily lives and can be incorporated into daily activities provided for the children throughout the day. For example:
    - At lunch time, soothing instrumental music will promote a relaxing background for this busy time.
    - At nap time, soft or easy-listening music and lullabies will set the stage for a quiet time.
2. A variety of music that reflects different cultures, styles, and rhythms should be introduced and played throughout the day.
3. A variety of instruments should always be available for children to explore and play with.

Musical activities should promote freedom of expression and creativity. The children should freely sing, play, and move as they want to.

Music and Movement Environment Checklist

- record player
- tape recorder
- CD player
- action or quiet music tapes
- streamers
- scarves
- finger play books
- variety of records, music tapes, or CDs

Musical Instruments

- tambourines
- maracas
- cymbals
- rhythm sticks sets
- sand blocks
- wrist bells
- ankle bells
- hand bells
- pianos
- triangles
- cowbell
- xylophone

Art Center

Art can be everywhere and is in all that we do. Art should not only be planned but available as an activity choice every day. A wide variety of materials and equipment should be provided and located within children's reach to stimulate creativity and independence.

1. Allow children to explore on their own. Children need the freedom to experiment and discover new things for themselves.

2. Do not make a model for children to copy or finish a project for them.

3. Do not use coloring pages. Children need the freedom and opportunity to express their creativity.

4. Focus all art projects on the process of doing and not on the final product.

5. Do not tell children that they could do a better job. Praise them for their efforts.

6. Display the children's art attractively and with respect throughout the room at children's eye level. Children need to know their work is valued and respected by others.

7. Always talk to children about what they are doing and be there if they need your assistance.

8. Always provide materials that children can explore in many different ways.

9. Plan to introduce different art projects throughout the week, but provide opportunities for repetitions of favorite art projects as well.

10. Make sure art supplies are nontoxic and age appropriate.

11. It is important to provide and maintain a stocked and organized art center. Children need to feel secure and encouraged to explore and learn.

Art Center Environment Checklist

- easels
- easel clips
- plastic cups or containers
- plastic bows
- different sizes of paintbrushes
- trays for fingerpainting and paint trays
- watercolors
- tempera paint / finger paint
- plastic table cover for messy activities
- different types of paper (construction paper, tissue paper, manila, etc.)
- safety scissors / scissors rack
- storage containers
- glue or glue sticks / paste
- markers and crayons
- yarn
- food coloring
- flour, salt, and oil for play dough
- cleanup supplies (soap, sponges, buckets, paper towels)

- plastic covers for floors
- different materials for collage
- hole puncher
- staples / staplers
- art sponges
- nonhardening clay
- templates
- white/colored chalk
- pipe cleaners
- colored pencils
- craft sticks
- stamps
- nature material such as leaves, flowers, rocks, and sand for different art projects
- smocks for children and teachers
- permanent markers for teachers
- writing notepads

Do not forget to set up your art center based on the age group of children and their developmental stages. Scissors are not appropriate for toddlers, because they may not have the motor skills necessary to operate scissors and they might cut themselves.

Manipulative Area

Playing with manipulative toys helps children to improve social skills, language development, creativity, and development of fine motor skills. A variety of manipulative toys (table toys) should be available every day for individual or small groups of children to use.

1. Always offer duplicates of toys (especially with toddlers) to avoid unnecessary disputes.

Be careful to select toys for children that are age appropriate and meet the different levels of development. Children need to be challenged, but they also need to feel successful in order to learn with confidence.

2. Rotate toys to maintain interest.

3. Always provide manipulative toys that have a variety of skill levels (simple to difficult). Younger children should start playing with puzzles that contain bigger and fewer pieces. As they acquire and master new skills, you gradually increase the size and amount of pieces of the puzzles.

4. Make sure all toys are safe and age appropriate for the children in your care. Toys for younger children should not have any movable parts or be small enough to fit in their mouth.

5. Talk to children about what they are doing and show children how to use the toys appropriately.

6. Manipulative toys should be displayed on low shelves, within children's reach, to promote independence and freedom of choice.

7. Label the toy containers and shelves with pictures to help children be independent and keep the classroom organized.

Manipulative Toys Checklist

- plastic building bricks
- puzzles
- pegs and peg-boards
- small blocks
- large beads and strings
- rings and laces
- giant plastic nuts and bolts
- puzzle blocks
- hammer pegs
- pounding benches
- snap beads
- chain links
- lacing frames
- table blocks
- sorting boards
- wooden picture dominoes
- self-help skills dressing pads (snapping, lacing, zipping, etc.)

Sensory Experiences

Children have a natural curiosity to explore. They learn by touching, feeling, and using other senses to discover the world around them. Sensory experiences promote:

- language development
- creativity
- ability to socialize
- ability to follow directions
- development of fine motor skills
- learning about cause and effect

1. Offer sensory experiences as part of the daily activity plan.
2. Sensory activities can be incorporated into any other activity area, including science, library, art, and dramatic play.

Sensory Activities

- sand and water play
- play dough, Silly Putty®, clay
- texture boards
- texture papers
- texture books
- food experiences
- different types of paint
- smelly jars
- sound canisters

Science Area

Science and opportunities for science activities are everywhere in the environment that surrounds us. Science activities can be as simple as an outside walk to observe nature or manipulating play dough.

1. Plan a science experience every day.
2. Children should be exposed to different opportunities to interact with their environment, such as listening to nature or instruments' sounds, and feeling different textures around their environment like play dough, paint, sand, rocks, etc.
3. All science activities should provide opportunities for children to explore with hands-on experience.
4. Allow adequate amount of time for children to fully explore and work on science experiences.
5. Provide a variety of exciting and interesting materials and equipment for children to discover the world around them.
6. Always encourage children's curiosity and praise them for their discoveries and accomplishments.
7. Get involved in children's play. Be there to enhance their experiences by asking questions or offering other types of materials and equipment that will extend their imagination and creativity.

Good Tips for Planning Science Activities

- Make sure the activities you offer are appropriate for the age group you are working with.

- All science activities should meet children's interests and stimulate learning and creativity.

- Before starting your science experience, make sure you have all the materials and equipment you need within easy reach.

- Some science experiences require adult supervision. Be there to assist the children whenever necessary.

- To have more control of the activity, you should work with a small number of children at one time. It is important that all children participating in the activity have a hands-on chance to explore and discover the experience.

- Talk and listen to children during the entire science activity.

- Observe and assess the activity for any changes that might be necessary for improving future activities.

Assessing Your Activities

It is important that you take the time to observe and assess your entire science activity. Having an open mind to self-criticism and the positive criticism of others will help you to make necessary changes.

Modifying your activities to meet children's needs and interests will give them the opportunity to learn with confidence and success.

Questions for Assessing Your Activities

- Does the activity meet the needs and interests of the children?
- Does the activity promote learning and stimulate creativity?
- Is the activity age appropriate and does it meet the development levels of the children?
- Do I provide enough materials and equipment for all the children? Do the materials offered enhance the activity?
- Do any changes need to be made to ensure that future activities are better?

CAUTION *To have a successful science experience, you need to choose activities that are safe and interesting so that children can and will participate.*

Science Environment Checklist

- magnets
- pets
- sand
- water
- snails
- shells
- rocks
- sponges
- measuring cups
- play dough
- sink-and-float objects
- activities to experience such natural elements as rain, snow, sun, wind, etc.
- skeletons/pictures of the human body

- variety of sound-producing objects/instruments
- cooking supplies: oil, water, food coloring, baking soda, salt, etc.
- vegetables
- glue
- corn starch
- fish tank
- animal and bugs
- plants
- seeds
- potting soil
- egg cartons
- eyedroppers
- microscope
- magnifying glass

Dramatic Play

Dramatic or pretend play can be anything that a child's imagination allows. Dramatic play is fantasy, adventure, professional careers, puppet shows, singing, acting, dancing, and much more.

As children engage in dramatic play, they are learning and improving their ability to

- socialize (how to interact with others)
- follow directions
- work through problems
- share
- take turns
- try on adult roles
- develop language skills

1. Organize your dramatic play area with exciting and interesting materials and equipment to encourage children to explore and to have fun.

2. Dramatic play activities and ideas should promote cooperation and socialization.

   Ravi, I am fixing breakfast. Would you help me set up the table?

3. Observe children playing to ensure their safety and prevent them from engaging in dangerous play or situations.

4. Give children adequate time to engage and carry out their play.

5. Allow children to play without an adult interaction. It is important for children to develop the ability to socialize with their peers.

6. You can enhance children's play by participating and also asking questions to extend their imagination.

   Mr. Salesman, can you help me find a beautiful dress for my birthday party?

   Kelly, what are we going to have for lunch today?

7. Help children learn words to express their feelings and ideas, and to talk about their play.

Prop Boxes Ideas

Prop boxes are used to enhance children's play by extending their imagination and creativity. Prop boxes are easy to put together and can be very inexpensive. Here are some creative ideas to help you find appropriate materials and equipment for your prop boxes.

- Take the time to look around your facility for things that are already available.
- Ask your children's parents for donations. Let the parents know the things you need for your program.
- Another great idea is to spend some time at local yard sales. You will be surprised with the variety of items and good bargains you can find.
- Rotate your prop boxes according to the theme or activity being implemented in your curriculum.

Jewelry and Accessory Prop Box

- bracelets
- eyeglasses
- rings
- sunglasses
- necklaces
- scarves

Office Prop Box

- typewriter
- small tables and chairs
- paper
- eraser
- pencils and pencil sharpeners
- notepads
- telephones
- pens
- markers
- crayons

Gas Station Prop Box

- cars
- trucks
- cash register
- hats
- tires
- gas tank
- work clothes
- plastic containers
- play people

Grocery Store Prop Box

- cash register
- play money
- pencils
- markers and crayons
- paper
- work clothes
- play food
- paper bags
- plastic bottles

Doctor's Office Prop Box

- stethoscope
- play syringe
- pretend thermometer
- Band-Aids®
- gauze
- face mask
- doctor's and nurse's work clothes
- telephone
- markers and crayons
- notepads
- cash register
- eye chart

Dramatic Play Environment Checklist

- hats
- clothes
- shoes
- jewelry
- unbreakable mirrors
- purses and wallets
- scarves
- sunglasses, etc.
- child-sized tables and chairs
- cooking utensils
- multicultural dolls
- shoes
- refrigerator, stove
- washer and dryer
- dishes, pots, and pans
- dress-up clothes
- books
- brooms and mops
- telephone
- play food
- puppets and puppet stand
- doll houses and high chairs
- play people
- and much, much more!

CHAPTER 7

Remember to be safe! All equipment and materials used in the prop boxes should be in good condition, meet the different levels of children's development, and be age appropriate.

abc

Block Area

Block building is a fun and an exciting learning activity for children of all ages. By playing with blocks, children learn new concepts and improve their ability to

- socialize with friends
- learn concepts as big and small; thick and thin; soft and hard
- develop language
- learn about cause and effect
- develop math skills
- solve problems
- take turns
- share
- cooperate
- develop hand-eye coordination skills

1. When setting up the block area, remember to make it organized, well stocked (not cluttered), attractive, and inviting.

2. The size of your block area should determine the number of children who are allowed to work comfortably at one time.

3. Make sure you provide other equipment and props that will extend children's imagination and enhance their play.

4. All blocks and other equipment should be safe, nontoxic, and age appropriate.

5. As with any other activity area, clear limits with simple rules must be established for the safety of the children.

   Blocks are for building and not for hitting.

   Buildings can only be as tall as the builder is.

 **Be consistent in following the rules. What is not acceptable today should not be acceptable tomorrow.**

6. Always supervise children and give them constant reminders of the rules.

7. Give children the space and freedom to engage in their own play. It is important that you allow children to discover, learn, and solve problems on their own.

8. Always observe children and know when to participate in their play. You can enhance their play by offering other equipment and props or by asking questions to extend their thinking.

   Mark, how can you make your garage bigger so the truck can come in?

   Here are some people for your house party, Kayla!

9. Shelves and containers should be properly labeled. Knowing where everything goes will make for easier cleanup times and children will learn concepts of sorting and classification.

10. Allow adequate time for children to engage and carry out their play.

11. Block building should be offered as a daily activity.

12. Rotate blocks and other equipment to maintain children's interest.

13. Always praise children for their good work and new accomplishments.

Block Area Environment Checklist

- hard unit blocks
- soft blocks
- Legos/Duplos
- animal props
- dollhouse furniture
- wooden barn
- transportation blocks
- people props
- traffic sign sets
- play mats
- waffle blocks
- cardboard blocks
- foam building blocks
- hollow blocks
- cars, trucks, motorcycles
- cash register
- puppets
- and much, much more!

Library or Book Area

Materials and Equipment

- soft chairs
- rocking chairs
- pillows
- bookshelves
- puppets
- flannelboard stories
- writing tools

- homemade books

- paper

- multicultural books

- duplicates of favorite books

- books about feelings

- books about friends

- books about families

- books about weather, etc.

- pictures of familiar things

- family pictures

- books with audiotapes

Outdoor Activities

Children love outdoor activities because they love to be outside. It is like being free and able to do whatever they want. Outdoor activities are as important as indoor activities. The outdoor environment should be full of exciting and fun things to do. Children must be able to move freely and release their energy in constructive ways.

1. All the activities that you do inside of the classroom can and should be done outdoors.

2. Take advantage of what nature has to offer to provide children with healthy and exciting ways to explore and learn.

   - On a beautiful spring day, have the children take their nap outdoors.

   - Go for a nature walk as often as you can. Give children the opportunity to discover for themselves. Observe children carefully and take notes of their findings and accomplishments.

   - The outdoor environment is also great for group times. Whether you read books, sing songs, or exercise to music, being outside can help make the activity exciting and fun for the whole group.

3. Check the outdoor environment for safety hazards before starting your activities.

4. All outdoor equipment should be safe and in good condition.

5. Adults should always be alert and involved in children's play. Interacting with the children is a good way of keeping them safe and to have fun at the same time.

6. Set clear limits with simple rules for the children and be consistent following them. Children need to know which activities and behaviors are acceptable and which are not in order to play safe and have respect for others.

7. Constant supervision of the children and frequent reminders of the rules are always necessary to keep the children safe.

   Paul, I need you to sit down on the swing.

   Tania, sand belongs in the sandbox.

8. Be aware and constantly take a number count of the children in your care while playing outside.

9. Make children feel responsible by assigning them small tasks.

   Alex, today you will be responsible for passing out the paper cups to your friends. It is a hot day and we need to make sure everybody is drinking water.

10. Get everything you need for outside play before going outdoors (water, tissues, paper towels, paper cups, broom, first aid kit, attendance sheet, etc.) to avoid leaving other staff out of ratio or the children unattended. When assisting a child in the bathroom, make sure the other children are safe and properly cared for.

11. Children's clothing should be appropriate for the weather and comfortable for freedom of movement.

12. Be flexible when planning outdoor activities. Let children choose between activities you offer and their own play.

13. You can enhance outdoor play by participating in children's play, and providing interesting materials and equipment for children to explore.

Outdoors Play Environment Checklist

- ropes
- swings
- cardboard boxes
- softball and bats
- tricycles
- wagons
- beanbags and targets
- rocking boats
- gardening tools
- woodworking tools
- cars, sand trucks
- sand tools
- outside chalk
- balance beams
- tape recorder / CD player
- tapes / CDs
- streamers
- instruments
- water and sand table
- water and sand toys
- parachutes
- balls
- slides
- bowling balls and pins
- ring toss
- stompers
- small table and chairs

Quiet Area: A Place to Escape

Sometimes, all that goes on in the environment can overwhelm youngsters and create tension among the children in the classroom. Children need time and space to get away, to catch their breath, and to slow down for a while. It is important that you incorporate cozy places in your environment, creating a nurturing atmosphere.

1. Quiet areas are small and cozy places, where one or two children can go and rest for a while.

2. Quiet areas should be places that children can go to on their own when they wish. These areas should not be used for time-outs or to punish children for their actions and behavior.

You can create soft and warm places with very basic things such as:

- soft pillows
- soft couch
- fluffy mats
- pictures
- books
- dolls
- blankets
- big cardboard boxes

Anything that creates a soothing environment can be used to establish a quiet area. Use your imagination!

For additional information on quality child care, visit our Web site at **http://www.earlychilded.delmar.com**

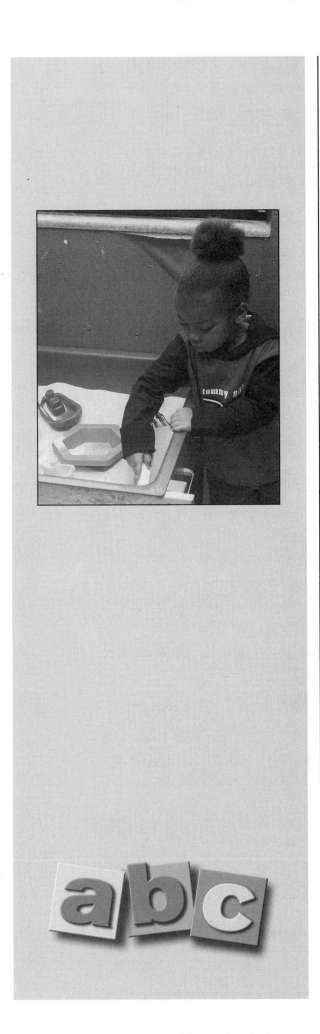

Chapter 8

Curriculum

- Goals and Objectives of the Curriculum
- Evaluating Your Curriculum
- Guidelines for Appropriate Activities
- Activity Planning
- Evaluating Your Activities

To develop the right curriculum, it is important that you take the time to observe the children in your care.

Children are unique individuals, with different needs and interests. They also are likely to be at different levels of development. By observing the children in your care you will be able to gather all the information necessary to help you develop and implement a curriculum that is appropriate and relevant for the lives of young children.

Goals and Objectives of the Curriculum

An appropriate curriculum provides activities and experiences that promote and enhance children's social, emotional, cognitive, language and communication, and physical development.

- Social: The curriculum helps children feel comfortable and secure in their environment and helps children develop positive relationships with adults and peers.
- Emotional: The curriculum helps children build positive self-esteem and sets the stage for children to learn with confidence and success.
- Cognitive: The curriculum helps children become confident explorers and learners by providing opportunities for children to use all their senses to explore the entire environment, develop new concepts and skills, and develop their thinking skills.
- Physical: The curriculum helps children develop and increase large and small muscle abilities and skills.

As you plan your curriculum, be sure to provide opportunities for children to undertake active exploration and develop positive interactions with adults, peers, and the environment.

1. An appropriate curriculum should provide opportunities for children to work on their present level of development. By increasing the difficulty and complexity of an activity, your program should foster opportunities that will challenge the children to master new skills.

2. The curriculum should be planned based on children's needs and interests.

3. The curriculum should provide opportunities for language development. Children need to feel comfortable to express their ideas, feelings, and discoveries.

4. The curriculum should provide a variety of hands-on activities and experiences. Children should be able to explore and experiment with all materials and equipment for themselves.

5. The materials used to implement the activities of your curriculum should be real and provide a variety of experiences.

6. The curriculum should involve children in appropriate activity areas such as:

- dramatic play
- manipulatives
- creative art
- blocks
- science/sensory
- movement
- group times
- language/library

7. All the learning activities should be concrete and relevant for children. Children need to relate the activities being implemented in your curriculum to their daily experiences. For example, if the children in your care are not from a place that snows, you should not plan activities like playing in the snow or building a snowman. Because the children are not exposed to the snow, the activity will not be relevant to their lives. In this case, a more appropriate way to introduce snow to your children is through weather books, videos, and science/sensory activities such as playing with shaved ice.

For more information on appropriate curricula for young children, please read *Developmentally Appropriate Practices in Early Childhood Program Serving Children from Birth through Age 8,* edited by Sue Bredekamp (Washington, DC: National Association for the Education of Young Children, 1992) and C. Gestwicki's *Developmentally Appropriate Practice: Curriculum and Development in Early Education,* 2nd ed. (Clifton Park, NY: Delmar Learning, 1999).

Evaluating Your Curriculum

After developing and implementing your curriculum with the children in your care, it is important that you take time to evaluate the curriculum for any necessary changes or improvements. Here are four important questions you should answer in your curriculum assessment:

1. Is the curriculum effective? Is it accomplishing the goals you expected to achieve?
2. Are the goals and objectives of your program being implemented?
3. Is the curriculum relevant to the children's needs and interests? Is it meaningful to their lives?
4. Is the curriculum based on children's present levels of development? Are the children successful in their learning experiences?

Another way to evaluate your curriculum is through receiving feedback from the children, families, and the people who directly work with you. Being honest with yourself and having an open mind toward constructive criticism can help you make the changes necessary to improve your curriculum.

Guidelines for Appropriate Activities

1. Activities are relatively easy to do and meet the development levels of the children. Children need to be successful in order to be confident and active learners.

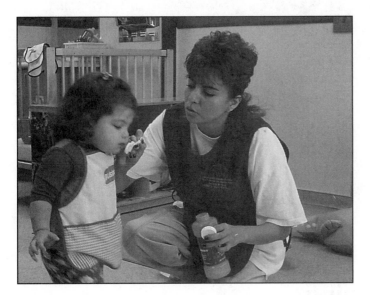

2. The activities are noncompetitive. Children should not compete against their peers, but be able to feel successful by their own accomplishments.

3. Activities have no right or wrong answers. Remember to always praise children for their efforts and accomplishments.

4. Children need repetitions of the same activities in order to master concepts and skills.

5. New activities should be introduced as often as possible. Observe the children in your care to find out their developmental levels and set up new goals to be accomplished as you introduce new activities.

6. Activities should provide opportunities for socialization. Children will learn how to share and take turns by having positive relationships with peers and adults.

7. The focus of an activity should be on the process of doing it, not on the final product.

8. Most of your daily schedule should foster activities that are child directed. Children should be free to choose their own activities (free play) and engage in their own play.

Activity Planning

Things to Remember When Planning Activities

1. What is the purpose or goal of activity planned?

2. How many children will be able to participate in the activity? (group size)

3. How much preparation time is required?

4. What materials are needed to implement the activity?

5. Will the children have access to the materials?

6. How will you introduce the activity (art, circle time, outside play, etc.)?

7. How will you extend the activity into the other activity areas?

Example of an Activity

Time of Year: Fall

Group activity: Nature walk

Purpose: Language skills—Talk about fall changes in the environment.

Listening skills—Listen to the sounds of the leaves falling or being stepped on.

Art: Collage preparation, using the leaves collected on the nature walk.

Gross motor: Free movement—flying like the leaves or the birds in the air.

Evaluating Your Activities

1. Did the activity go the way it was planned?

2. Was the purpose of the activity achieved? If not, why? What could be done in the future to change or enhance the activity?

3. Was the activity based on children's needs and interests? Were the children interested in the activity?

4. Was the activity meaningful and relevant to the children?

5. Did the activity set the children for a successful learning experience?

6. Were the materials and equipment used age appropriate and safe for the children to manipulate?

7. Did the activity provide opportunities for hands-on experience?

8. Did the activity foster children's independence and autonomy?

9. Did the activity foster socialization?

There are many different books on appropriate activities for young children that can help you prepare your daily activity plan. Take some time to visit your local library to research early childhood activity books.

Briggs, P., Pilot, T., & Bagby, J. (2001). *Early childhood activities for creative educators.* Clifton Park, NY: Delmar Learning.

Green, M. D. (1998). *Themes with a difference: 228 new activities for young children.* Clifton Park, NY: Delmar Learning.

Green, M. D. (1998). *Not! the same old activities for early childhood.* Clifton Park, NY: Delmar Learning.

Green, M. D. (1996). *474 science activities for young children.* Clifton Park, NY: Delmar Learning.

Hamilton, D. S. (1990). *Resources for creative teaching in early childhood education.* Clifton Park, NY: Delmar Learning.

Herr, J. (2001). Creative learning activities for young children. Clifton Park, NY: Delmar Learning.

Herr, J. (2000). *Creative resources for the early childhood classroom* (3rd ed.). Clifton Park, NY: Delmar Learning.

Herr, J., & Swim, T. (2002). *Creative resources for infants and toddlers* (2nd ed.). Clifton Park, NY: Delmar Learning.

Herr, J. (1998). *Creative resources of art, brushes, buildings.* Clifton Park, NY: Delmar Learning.

Herr, J. (1998). *Creative resources of birds, animals, seasons, holidays.* Clifton Park, NY: Delmar Learning.

Herr, J. (1998). *Creative resources of colors, food, plants & occupations.* Clifton Park, NY: Delmar Learning.

 For additional information on quality child care, visit our Web site at **http://www.earlychilded.delmar.com**

Chapter 9

Guidance and Discipline

- Guidance and Discipline
- A Sense of Structure
- Some Important Guidelines to Remember

Guidance and Discipline

Care providers play an important role in guiding children to develop self-discipline. Consequently, it is extremely important that child care providers understand the whole process of child development to know what to expect of children and why. By understanding how children grow and learn, child care providers can use positive guidance tools to help children with the many challenges they face on a daily basis.

The role of a child care provider is to guide and discipline children toward having acceptable behaviors and never, in any situation, to punish children for their actions. Care providers should never

- use corporal punishment (spanking, pinching, or shaking the child)
- separate a child from adult sight or contact
- confine a child in closets, boxes, or similar places
- humiliate a child in front of peers or family
- verbally abuse a child
- force a child in extended periods of time-outs
- deprive a child of meals and snacks
- neglect a child's needs

Tips for Your Guidance and Discipline Policy

- Always notify parents of changes in their child's behavior or if a pattern of behavior develops that is disruptive to the program.
- Set up parent-teacher conferences to talk about discipline situations and how they should be handled.
- Determine what to do if the child's disruptive behavior persists in your program.

A Sense of Structure

Young children are little people growing up in a big world, facing new challenges and adventures every day of their lives. Children need to feel safe and comfortable with their environment in order to make sense of the world and everything that goes on around them. A structured environment will facilitate and provide comforting and familiar surroundings for children to explore and learn with success.

You can create a structured environment for the children in your care in many different ways:

1. Keep your schedule and routines consistent. The repetition of routines and activities will help children to know what is going to take place next. When children can predict events, their anxiety is eliminated and they feel comfortable and safe in their environment.

2. Make rules and set limits that are clear and consistent.

   Mark, when you drop your toys on the floor, you need to pick them up.

   We draw on the paper and not on the wall.

   Thelma, if you want to play in the water table, you need to go wash your hands.

   Make sure you follow through with the rules and limits that you have set. Children are active learners and as they become more independent, most likely they will put your rules and limits to the test.

3. Be there to remind the children of what they are supposed to do, no matter how many times they break the rules.

4. Tell children what they can do, instead of what they cannot do. Use positive words.

   Instead of: *No running!*

   You can say: *Use your walking feet indoors!*

   Instead of: *Do not scream!*

   You can say: *Use your inside voice!*

   Instead of: *Do not climb on the chair!*

   You can say: *We climb on the climber and sit on the chair!*

5. Focus on a child's actions, not on the child.

   Instead of: *Good boy, Logan! You cleaned up the spill all by yourself.*

   You can say: *Good job, Logan! I like the way you cleaned up the spill all by yourself.*

Instead of: *Look at all these toys on the floor, Jenna. You are a messy girl!*

You can say: *Jenna you are busy playing today! Just remember to pick up all the toys when you are finished playing with them.*

6. Give children autonomy to choose. Like adults, children want to feel independent and be able to make their own decisions. When giving choices to children, make sure all of their options are acceptable no matter what they choose.

   Do you want to lie down with your blanket or without your blanket?

   Do you want to go potty by yourself or do you want me to help you?

   What colors do you want, red or green?

   What would you like to drink, milk or apple juice?

 In all the situations above, at least two acceptable choices were offered. Children will be able to feel competent and successful by making their own choices and knowing that you will accept them.

7. The choices you give to children should guide them to respond appropriately.

   Instead of: *Would you like to change your diaper?* (Diaper changing is not a choice, it is a necessity.)

   You can say: *It is time to change your diaper. Do you want to hold the diaper for me?* (Remember always to provide situations that allow for acceptable choices.)

   Instead of: *Do you want to pick up the toys now?*

   You can say: *It is cleanup time! Do you want to pick up the toys in the house area or in the block area?* (Both are acceptable choices.)

8. Always respect children's choices and accept their feelings. As children exercise their autonomy to choose, it is necessary that you provide many opportunities for children to say no. Here are two examples:

   Teacher: *Do you want me to read you a book?*

   Child: *No.*

Teacher: *Okay. Maybe I can read you a book later.*

Teacher: *I know you are tired because you did not sleep well last night, but I cannot let you hurt your friends! Would you like me to hold you?*

Child: *No.*

Teacher: *Okay. Let us see if we can find a quiet place for you to rest.*

9. Provide opportunities for children to make rules.

   What do you think should happen if we leave the toys all over the floor?

   How should we pick the helper for lunchtime today?

   What do you think should happen when you hurt your friends?

Make sure to write the rules down as the children give them to you. Also remember to hang the rules at children's eye level. Whenever possible, use pictures to help children who cannot read.

10. Children need constant reminders of the rules.

    Use your walking feet inside.

    Keep the water in the water table.

    Use your inside voice in the building.

    We draw on the paper and not on the wall.

    Wash your hands after going to the bathroom.

11. Discourage inappropriate behavior. Children need to understand the consequences of their actions:

    Christopher, I know you are angry because your mom just left, but I will not let you hurt yourself or your friends. I will hold you until you feel better.

    Tina, you need to pick up all the pieces of the puzzle you dropped on the floor, or you are not allowed to play with the puzzles anymore today.

    Sometimes ignoring the child's behavior, will cause the child to stop for not getting the response she is looking for. For example:

    • Children using inappropriate or not so nice words

    • Children imitating adults or other children

12. Redirect children to acceptable activities and behaviors.

 Child: *Parker is jumping up and down on the sofa.*

 Teacher: *Parker, I am going to take you over to a soft and open area where you can jump up and down safely.*

 Child: *Gretchen hit Pedro because she wants a car.*

 Teacher: *I know you like to play with cars, but I will not let you hurt your friend so you can have the car. Let us see if Pedro is okay and then we are going to look for a car just for you.*

 Child: *I don't want to take a nap.*

 Teacher: *It is okay not to be tired, Alexa. Let's go to the book area and read some books while the other children are asleep.*

13. Praise children for their good behavior!

 • Children feel good about themselves when they feel good about what they do. Adults can help children feel successful by praising them for their efforts and good behavior.

 • When children are acknowledged and praised with specific feedback for what they have done, most likely they will repeat the good behavior over and over again.

- Other children will also imitate good behaviors.

I like the way you washed your hands!

Thank you for picking up your toys!

I like when you share the blocks with your friends!

14. Be a role model to children. Children also learn what is acceptable and what is not acceptable by watching you. It is important that you be a role model to children by respecting and accepting the feelings and opinions of others.

15. Use "I" messages to make it personal between you and the child.

   I need you to leave your coat on. It is very cold outside and I do not want you to get sick.

16. Model the use of good manners.

   Please pass me the rice, Nicholas. Thank you!

17. Recognize and respect children's feelings.

   I know you are sad because you want your mommy. Maybe if I show you some family pictures you will feel better.

18. You can use rewards to reinforce good actions or behaviors. The reward must be given because of something good that the child has done, and not used as a way of getting children to do what you want.

Some Important Guidelines to Remember

1. Accept others' opinions and be open to positive criticism.

   Lauren, maybe if you talk with a lower tone of voice, children will not be afraid of you.

2. Leave your problems at home! Children need your total dedication. Take a few minutes to relax and forget about outside problems before coming to work and have a great day!

3. Treat others as you want to be treated.

4. Promote independence, but be there to help children when they need your assistance.

5. Help children to express their feelings by letting them know how you feel.

   When you scream in the classroom, I get upset because it hurts my ears.

6. Take good care of yourself so children can learn good health habits.

7. Give children and other adults lots of TLC—tender loving care.

For additional information on quality child care, visit our Web site at **http://www.earlychilded.delmar.com**

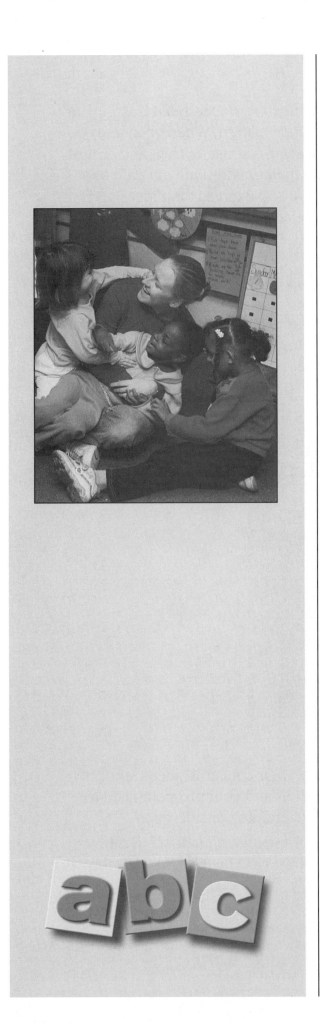

Chapter 10

Communication

Communication

Good communication is the most effective way to build trusting and lasting relationships with families and children. When good and constructive communication is established, a sense of trust and security develops. Parents feel safe leaving their children in your care and they know that they will be able to freely express their ideas and concerns about your program and the care that you offer.

How to Communicate with Parents

It is important that care providers are willing to hear and work with parents for the benefit of their children. Working as a team will not only facilitate and support the children's development, but also will create constructive communication between their home and your program.

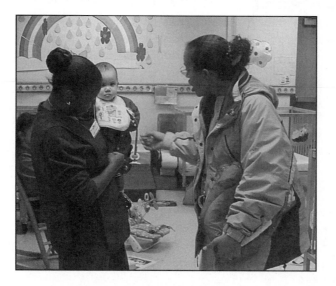

1. Listen to parents.
    - Parents want to be heard. Their concerns, ideas, and opinions about their children and your program need to be freely expressed and taken into consideration.
    - Parents want to make sure they have made the right decision by choosing the best care facility available for their children.

- Parents need to feel comfortable and secure about leaving their children in your care. Parents want the assurance that the people caring for the children, the environment, and daily experiences are all going to have positive influences on the lives of their children.

2. Think of ways that you can help your parents deal with their concerns, ideas, or opinions. For example, Mrs. Ann thinks that her child is ready for potty training, but Claudia does not show any interest in being potty trained. The caregiver should

   - offer Mrs. Ann some literature on potty training
   - set up a potty training conference with Mrs. Ann to discuss and determine if Claudia is physically and emotionally ready to be potty trained

3. Express your ideas and opinions in a meaningful and positive way.

4. Be sensitive to the parents' needs and wants.

5. Make sure that when offering help you give your parents the freedom to accept or not. For example, the caregiver wants to help Mrs. Ann understand how potty teaching works:

Mrs. Ann, I know you want Claudia to be potty trained right now, but it will be much easier for Claudia when the time is right for her. She needs to be emotionally ready to know what is being expected of her and physically able to do the tasks she needs to do. We want potty training to be a positive and successful learning experience for your daughter. Do you still want to continue trying?

Sharing Information

1. Daily feedback sheets are an excellent way to provide information about children's daily experiences and activities while they are in your care. Daily feedback sheets should contain information about:

    - sleeping patterns
    - toileting/diapering
    - eating habits
    - special activities or experiences
    - caregiver comments or concerns

    Appendix C contains a sample daily feedback sheet.

2. Share children's developmental stages with their parents.

3. Share information about developmental skills that the child has acquired or is working on. For example:

    Danny is saying a few words. (skill acquired)

    Help Danny with language development through books, songs, and finger plays. (developmental task)

Parents' Resource File

A parents' resource file is a good idea to assist parents with finding developmentally appropriate materials and information they need to help stimulate their child's growth and development at home.

- Make materials and information from the parents' resource file available on a lending basis.
- Welcome parents to borrow any of the materials for a period of time.
- Encourage parents to contribute to the resource file with ideas, suggestions, and donations of developmentally appropriate materials.

Parents' Resource File Material and Equipment

- ideas for homemade toys
- toys that teach specific skills
- literature on toilet training, guidance and discipline, appropriate activities, etc.

- science/sensory books
- indoor/outdoor activity books
- receipt books
- play dough and fingerpainting recipes
- recorded tapes with songs, stories, and children's voices
- flannelboard stories
- addresses of parenting support groups
- contact information for state and national organizations on child development
- other useful information, such as newspaper or magazine articles
- books and tapes on health, safety, discipline, divorce, and other parenting topics

Setting up a Parent-Teacher Conference

1. Identify the reason or purpose of conference.
2. Notify the parents of the conference as soon as possible.
3. Find out the day and time that is convenient for the parents to come in.
4. Plan the conference ahead of time.
5. Make sure you collect any material or evidence that you will need to share with the parents during the conference (progress checklist, assessments, communication forms, etc.).
6. Identify goals to be accomplished.

The Conference

1. Before the parents' arrival, make sure you have everything set up to start.

2. At parents' arrival, start the conference by establishing a relaxing atmosphere between both parties. You can start by talking about your families, past or future events, or anything else that parents will feel comfortable talking about.

3. Acknowledge the parents' efforts in attending and participating in the conference.

4. Introduce the purpose of conference.

5. State your ideas and concerns.

6. Listen to the parents' responses. It is important that you allow parents to give you feedback and their input about the situation.

7. Provide any other information that might be relevant to the problem or situation.

8. Allow time for the parents' responses.

9. After the problem has been identified and accepted, assure the parents that everyone will work together as a team for the benefit of their child.

10. State ideas or suggestions that you might have to help the problem or situation.

11. Ask the parents if they have any ideas or suggestions that can help address the problem or situation.

12. Make sure consistency between home and school is established. Whatever is done at home should also be done in your program.

13. After the conference, establish a time frame to try the suggested solutions for the problem or situation.

14. Decide if a follow-up conference at a later date is necessary to evaluate the child's progress or if the parents will be notified of child's progress on a regular basis.

15. To finish the conference make sure you have something positive about their child that you want to share with the parents:
    - Child's developmental progress
    - Developmental skills that the child has mastered or is working on.
    - Child's good thinking, behavior, etc.

Remember! Conferences do not have to always be about problems or negative situations. Parent will be delighted to simply sit down and hear about their child's progress or about your program. If parents initiate a conference, the procedure is much the same.

1. Listen carefully to parents.
2. Take their ideas, opinions, and concerns into consideration.
3. Be flexible and open to parents' wants and needs.
4. Think of ways you can help the parents.
5. Express your ideas and opinions in a sensitive and meaningful way.
6. Identify any goals to be accomplished.
7. Establish a time frame for goals to be evaluated.
8. Decide if another conference will be necessary to evaluate progress or reevaluate the goals.
9. Always finish your conference on a positive note. Let the parents know that continuing to work as a team will only benefit their child.
10. Give the parents all the support and love they need.

Ways to Promote Communication

1. Always have an open door policy in your program. Parents should be invited and encouraged to visit your program at any time.
2. Encourage parents to participate in the decisions made about their child's care.
3. Invite parents to have a special lunch with their child.
4. Ask parents to volunteer. You will be surprised by how much they have to contribute to your program.
5. Conduct regular open houses, which provide a good opportunity for parents to visit your program and have some time to play with their child.
6. Parent-teacher conferences can be an excellent time for a friendly talk.
7. A cookout or picnic will establish a relaxing atmosphere in which to get to know your parents better.

8. Newsletters can also be an excellent way of communicating with your parents. Some topic ideas for your newsletter include:

- special celebrations (birthdays, new siblings, etc.)
- special activities
- field trips
- names of new children and their families
- updates on policies and regulations
- articles on various child development subjects

9. Offer a suggestions and ideas box. Welcome parents to voice their opinions and concerns through written notes. This is a particularly good idea for parents who have a busy schedule and do not have the time to stop and talk.

Communicating with Children

When communicating with children, adults must use responsive language that has a positive influence in children's lives. Responsive language must convey that children are respected, accepted, and valued for who they are.

1. Use positive words when talking to children.

   Instead of: *No running!*

   You can say: *Use your walking feet indoors!*

2. Make sure the words you use to communicate are not too strong and offensive.

   Instead of: *Messy boy! You spilled all your milk on the floor.*

   You can say: *I know you want to tell your friends all about your field trip today, but you need to pay more attention where you place your milk on the table.*

3. Encourage independence and autonomy when communicating with children.

   Instead of: *Gabriella, it is time to clean up the art area. Put the crayons down.*

   You can say: *I notice you have been working hard on your picture, Gabriella. You can finish your picture while we clean up the other areas.*

4. Help children to express their feelings and ideas by giving them words if necessary.

   Instead of: *Close your mouth! No biting!*

   You can say: *I know you are upset because you want that toy, but I will not allow you to bite your friends. Biting hurts!*

5. Help children understand and accept other people's feelings.

   Instead of: *Adam, stop pushing Isaiah!*

   You can say: *Isaiah, you need to tell Adam that you do not like when he pushes you down. Pushing hurts!*

6. Use reason and logic to communicate with children.

   Instead of: *No. We are not going for a nature walk right now!*

   You can say: *There is a rainstorm coming our way and it will be here very soon. It will be safer for us to stay inside for now. Maybe after the rain is gone we can go on our nature walk!*

7. Model good manners while communicating with children.

   Instead of: *Give me the milk, Liana.*

   You can say: *Please pass me the milk, Liana. Thank you!*

8. Extend children's thinking by asking open-ended questions.

   Instead of: *What are you drawing in your picture?*

   You can say: *I like the colors you are using in your picture. Would you like to talk about your picture?*

   Instead of: *This is the way you put the puzzle together.*

   You can say: *How do you think we can put this puzzle together?*

9. Validate children's feelings and let them know that you care.

   Instead of: *Big girls don't cry!*

   You can say: *I know you are sad because you want your mommy. Would you like me to hold you for a while?*

10. Elaborate while communicating, so children will have a better understanding.

    Instead of: *No sand on the floor!*

    You can say: *Keep the sand on the sand table. We don't want our friend to slip over the sand on the floor and get hurt.*

11. Pay close attention and listen carefully to what children have to say at all times.

    Instead of: *Open your mouth! Don't talk like a baby.*

    You can say: *I need you to talk a little bit louder so I can hear you. Can you please tell me again what you just said?*

12. Let children know how you feel.

    Instead of: *Don't scream inside.*

    You can say: *Use your inside voice! It hurts my ears when you scream.*

13. Expand children's vocabulary by giving them words.

    Instead of: *More milk?*

    You can say: *Would you like to drink more milk?*

14. Always praise children for their efforts to communicate.

    Instead of: *Good boy, Miguel!*

    You can say: *Good job, Miguel! I like the way you asked me for more paint!*

Remember that communication between children and adults must be a two-way channel, where adults and children take the time to talk and listen to each other.

When positive communication is established, children feel comfortable and secure to express their feelings and ideas without fear of reproach or rejection. By properly communicating with children, adults can positively guide children to acceptable behaviors and teach them about self-respect and respect for others.

Ten Ways to Communicate with Children

1. Get as close to children as you can.

2. Look into their eyes.

3. Talk to children with a natural but firm tone of voice.

4. Use words that children can understand.

5. Be careful with strong and offensive words that can hurt children.

6. Recognize and accept children's feelings.

7. Give children words that can help them to express their feelings.

8. Help children understand the feelings of others.

9. Show children that you care and that you are there for them.

10. Praise children for taking the time to talk.

For additional information on quality child care, visit our Web site at **http://www.earlychilded.delmar.com**

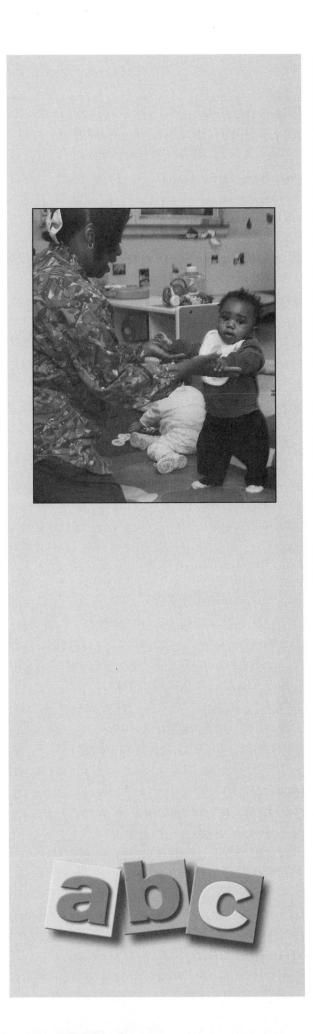

Chapter 11

The Role of a Caregiver

- The Role of a Caregiver
- What Responsive Caregivers Do

The Role of a Caregiver

With the increasing number of parents having to take jobs outside of their homes, children are spending more time at child care facilities. Parents are being forced to rely on outside care, hoping that their children will be cared for with love and respect.

High-quality child care is in great demand. Parents are not just looking for child care facilities that only meet the minimum standards or the basic needs of their children. Parents want a strong and reliable program where caring adults are implementing developmentally appropriate practices.

Child care professionals play an important role in the lives of young children. Our role is to meet all children's needs and promote their physical, social, emotional, and cognitive development in a supportive, healthy, and safe environment.

Being a child care professional means being able to give all you have for the benefit of the children. Children need responsive adults who will love, protect, and offer them a wide world of excitement, challenges, and discoveries.

It is not easy to be a good child care provider. Accepting the responsibility of caring for other people's children and facilitating their development can sometimes be overwhelming and very stressful. You have chosen one of the most challenging careers to pursue.

Being a child care professional will give you the most gratifying feeling of accomplishment. Have you ever stopped to think about how a child feels when you help her deal with separation and anxieties? What about the smile in the child's face when you help him complete a puzzle?

I hope you have realized that your role as a care provider is a very special one. By being there for the children and providing daily positive experiences in their lives, you will most likely set the stage for a successful life.

What Responsive Caregivers Do

- Responsive caregivers accept each child and their families, regardless of their color, race, or religion.

- Responsive caregivers feel good about themselves and enjoy working with children.

- Responsive caregivers respect children's feelings and ideas.

  I know you are upset because you want to go outside right now. As soon as the rain stops, we can go for a nature walk and smell the fresh air after it rains!

- Responsive caregivers help children understand the feelings of others.

  Jada, you need to tell Marcus that you do not like when he pulls your hair. It hurts!

- Responsive caregivers express their own feelings and ideas to children.

  Use your inside voice indoors, Mya! It hurts my ears when you talk too loud.

- Responsive caregivers expand children's vocabulary by giving them words to express their feeling and ideas.

  Child: *No!*

  Teacher: *That is right, Mason! You need to tell him that pushing hurts.*

- Responsive caregivers promote independence and autonomy.

  It is okay if you do not want to paint a picture today, Rylan! What do you want to do now?

- Responsive caregivers recognize and identify children's needs and respond appropriately.

  It is almost time for Cody to wake up from his nap and I know he will be hungry. I am going to prepare his bottle now.

- Responsive caregivers take advantage of routines like feeding, diaper changing, or toileting to have a closer and more personal relationship with the children.

- Responsive caregivers always let children know they are proud of their growth and development.

- Responsive caregivers are always there for the children. They quickly respond to their needs and interests.

- Responsive caregivers use appropriate language to talk and guide children to acceptable behaviors.

- Responsive caregivers are patient and understanding. They know children need adults who support their independence and are there when help is needed.

- Responsive caregivers protect children but do not restrict them from adventures and discoveries.

- Responsive caregivers provide consistent routines and schedules allowing children to be empowered and in control. Children need to know what is expected of them and the choices that are available to them.

- Responsive caregivers set simple and clear rules to keep children safe.

  We sit on the swing and stand on the ground!

- Responsive caregivers consistently follow rules, limits, and consequences.

- Responsive caregivers focus on a child's behavior and not on the child.

  Instead of: *Good girl! You look so cute cleaning up the table all by yourself.*

  You can say: *Good job! I really like the way you are cleaning the table all by yourself.*

- Responsive caregivers assign tasks to children that will make them feel confident and successful.

  Jared, please pass out the napkins to your friends. Thank you!

- Responsive caregivers promote independence by allowing children to do things for themselves.

  Zoe, I need you to go wash your hands after going to the bathroom. Let me know if you need any help!

- Responsive caregivers allow children to practice and master new skills.

- Responsive caregivers always praise children for their efforts and accomplishments with specific feedback.

  Way to go Martin! You put your shoes on all by yourself.

- Responsive caregivers identify children's needs and interests and use that information to plan daily activities.

  I noticed the children playing dentist this whole week. I know they will love a field trip to a real dentist's office. They will have fun and a more realistic experience.

- Responsive caregivers observe children's play and identify any developmental changes needed in the environment.

  Dakota seems very frustrated playing with that puzzle. Maybe I should put out a puzzle with fewer pieces for her to work with and gradually increase the level of complexity of the puzzles.

- Responsive caregivers set up and maintain a safe and healthy environment for children to explore.

- Responsive caregivers provide an environment that is attractive, organized, and full of exciting things to do and discover.

- Responsive caregivers are always looking for materials and equipment that will enhance children's play.

  The shoe boxes that I got from the shoe store will be great for collecting different objects on our nature walk tomorrow.

- Responsive caregivers make sure that materials and equipment used are safe, nontoxic, and in good condition.

- Responsive caregivers organize and display materials and equipment within children's reach, promoting independence.

- Responsive caregivers label shelves and containers to help children know where everything goes.

- Responsive caregivers provide an environment that is organized and fully equipped with age-appropriate toys and materials for children to manipulate.

- Responsive caregivers provide a warm and caring environment for children. Children need to feel that they belong there.

- Responsive caregivers respect children and their families by hanging their pictures throughout the child care facility.

- Responsive caregivers rotate toys and equipment to maintain children's interests.

- Responsive caregivers plan daily activities that will promote the development of social, emotional, physical, language and communication, and cognitive skills.

  Social: Small group activities

  Emotional: Taking turns on the swing and sharing toys

  Physical: Outside play, dancing, and exercising

  Cognitive: Puzzles, books, and blocks

- Responsive caregivers provide activities and opportunities for children to use all their senses to explore and learn, such as nature walks and cooking experiences.

- Responsive caregivers provide a balanced schedule between indoor and outdoor activities.

- Responsive caregivers provide opportunities for free play. Children are free to choose between activities or engage in their own play.

- Responsive caregivers tell children what they can do instead of what they cannot do.

  The water table is open, but you can also go to the book area if you want to read books.

- Responsive caregivers allow for freedom of choice. Make sure you always offer at least two acceptable choices. (No matter what they choose, it will be acceptable either way.)

  Would you like to sing songs or read books?

- Responsive caregivers promote independence and autonomy.

  It is okay if you do not want to participate in group time right now. Maybe you will join us later.

- Responsive caregivers prepare children for transition times.

  We have a few more minutes to play before we put the toys away.

- Responsive caregivers take advantage of transition times to help children practice and master new skills.

  It is time to go outside! Please put on your jackets and hats.

- Responsive caregivers enhance children's play by engaging in their play.

  Dr. Lucas, I think I hurt my leg. Can you take a look at it for me?

- Responsive caregivers ask open-ended questions to extend children's thinking.

  What do you think a plant needs to grow, Linda?

- Responsive caregivers let children try to solve their own problems. Make sure you are always observing children's play to know when to step in to keep children safe.

- Responsive caregivers take into consideration individual needs and interests when planning activities.

  Xavier is really trying to use the scissors. I will provide more activities for him to practice like cutting play dough and old magazines.

- Responsive caregivers always interact with children.
- Responsive caregivers always evaluate their program and are open for changes.

  The children love the volcano experience. Maybe next time I will have a smaller group of children participate at one time. That way, they will not be bored waiting for their turn.

- Responsive caregivers communicate with other staff members about children's development and the program.
- Responsive caregivers maintain open and constructive communication with families to exchange information about their children and the program.

  Mrs. Brown, Aysha did not want to participate in the activities today. She seemed a little tired. Did she sleep well last night?

- Responsive caregivers maintain confidentiality, and only use any information about children and their families to benefit other children and the program.
- Responsive caregivers invite and encourage parents to visit the program and to participate in making decisions about their children's care.

  I think Jacob is ready to eat solid food. I will ask Jacob's mom how she feels about starting her son on a new diet.

- Responsive caregivers promote ways to keep parents informed about the program, such as a newsletter, bulletin boards, parents' resource file, etc.
- Responsive caregivers value children's work, which is attractively displayed in the child care facility at children's eye level.
- Responsive caregivers talk to children about their work.
- Responsive caregivers support the needs of children and their families.
- Responsive caregivers always seek ways of self-improvement (books, classes, workshops) on child development.

A responsive and professional caregiver is a person who nurtures the development of children's lives with love. It is important that every child care provider has the ultimate goal to give to children the best beginning in life. Helping children develop positive self-esteem in the first years of their lives will most likely set them up for success in the future.

It is not an easy job to work with children. Your words, actions, and attitudes toward life will greatly influence many children's lives and the way they face daily challenges and adventures. I honestly hope that you have decided to make the commitment to be an excellent responsive caregiver. Children are counting on it!

For additional information on quality child care, visit our Web site at **http://www.earlychilded.delmar.com**

Appendix A
National Child Care Organizations

The Administration for Children and Families (ACF)
370 L'Enfant Promenade SW
Washington, DC 20447
http://www.acf.dhhs.gov

The Child Care Food Program
U.S. Department of Agriculture
Washington, DC 20250
http://www.usda.gov/

The Children's Foundation
725 15th Street NW, Suite 505
Washington, DC 20005-2109
Phone: 202-347-3300
Fax: 202-347-3382
E-mail: info@childrensfoundation.net
http://www.childrensfoundation.net/

Education International (ACEI)
17904 Georgia Avenue, Suite 215
Olney, MD 20832
Phone: 301-570-2111
Toll Free: 1-800-423-3563
Fax: 301-570-2212
E-mail: aceihq@aol.com
http://www.udel.edu/bateman/acei

National Association for Family Day Care
P.O. Box 10373
Des Moines, IA 50306
Toll Free: 1-800-359-3817
E-mail: nafcc@nafcc.org
http://www.nafcc.org

National Association for the Education of Young Children (NAEYC)
1509 16th Street, NW
Washington, DC 20036-1426
http://www.naeyc.org

National Association of Child Care Professionals
P.O. Box 90723
Austin, TX 78709-0723
Phone: 512-301-5557
Toll Free: 1-800-537-1118
Fax: 512-301-5080
E-mail: admin@naccp.org
http://www.naccp.org

National Child Care Association
1016 Rosser Street
Conyers, GA 30012
Toll Free: 1-800-543-7161
http://www.nccanet.org/

National Child Care Information Center
243 Church Street, NW, 2nd Floor
Vienna, VA 22180
Toll Free: 1-800-616-2242
Fax: 1-800-716-2242
TTY: 1-800-516-2242
E-mail: info@nccic.org
http://www.nccic.org

National Head Start Association
1651 Prince Street
Alexandria, VA 22314
Phone: 703-739-0875
Fax: 703-739-0878
http://www.nhsa.org

National Resource Center for Health and Safety in Child Care
UCHSC at Fitzsimons
Campus Mail Stop F541
P.O. Box 6508
Aurora, CO 80045-0508
Toll Free: 1-800-598-KIDS
E-mail: natl.child.res.ctr@uchsc.edu
http://nrc.uchsc.edu

U.S. Department of Health and Human Services
200 Independence Avenue SW
Washington, DC 20201
Phone: 202-619-0257
Toll Free: 1-877-696-6775
E-mail: HHS.Mail@hhs.gov
http://www.hhs.gov

U.S. Small Business Administration
409 3rd Street SW
Washington, DC 20416
Toll Free: 1-800-U-ASK-SBA
http://www.sba.gov

USA National Child Abuse Hotline
For national child abuse information, call the Childhelp USA National Child Abuse Hotline (staffed 24 hours daily with professional crisis counselors):
1-800-4-A-CHILD or 1-800-2-A-CHILD (TDD)

Appendix B
State Contact Information

Alabama

Alabama Department of Human Resources
Childcare Subsidy Program
Family Assistance Division
50 North Ripley Street
Montgomery, AL 36104
Phone: 334-242-1773
Fax: 334-242-0513

Alabama Department of Children's Affairs
Head Start Collaboration Office
RSA Tower, 201 Monroe Street
Montgomery, AL 36130-2755
Phone: 334-223-0502
http://dca.state.al.us/osr/hsco.htm

Department of Human Resources
Office of Child Care Licensing Regulations,
Family Services
50 Ripley Street
Montgomery, AL 36130
Phone: 334-242-1425
Fax: 334-242-0939
http://www.dhr.state.al.us/fsd/licresdv.asp

Childcare Resource Network
P.O. Box 681025
Ft. Payne, AL 35968-1611
Phone: 256-845-8238
Fax: 256-845-6731

Alabama Department of Education
Attn.: State Director, Child Nutrition Programs
Gordon Persons Building
50 North Ripley Street, Room 5301
Montgomery, AL 36130-2101
Phone: 334-242-1988
Fax: 334-242-2475

Alabama Department of Human Resources
Division of Child Support
50 Ripley Street
Montgomery, AL 36130-1801
Phone: 334-242-9300
Fax: 334-242-0606
http://www.dhr.state.al.us/csed/default.asp

U.S. Small Business Administration
801 Tom Martin Drive, Suite 201
Birmingham, AL 35211
Phone: 205-290-7101
Fax: 205-290-7404

To report suspected child abuse in Alabama, call any sheriff's department or any county department of human resources office.

State Home Page: http://www.state.al.us/

State Child Care Home Page:
http://www.dhr.state.al.us/fad/child_care_sub.asp

Alaska

Alaska Department of Education and
Early Development
Division of Early Development
333 West 4th Avenue, Suite 220
Anchorage, AK 99501-2341
Phone: 907-269-4607
Fax: 907-269-4635

Alaska Department of Education and
Early Development
Head Start–State Collaboration Office
P.O. Box 112100
Juneau, AK 99811-2100
Phone: 907-465-4861
Fax: 907-465-8638
http://www.eed.state.ak.us/EarlyDev/headstart.html

Alaska Division of Family and Youth Services
P.O. Box 110630
Juneau, AK 99811-0630
Phone: 907-465-3207
Fax: 907-465-3397 or 907-465-3190
http://www.eed.state.ak.us/EarlyDev/licensing.html

Child Care Connection
P.O. Box 240008
Anchorage, AK 99524-0008
Phone: 907-563-1966
http://www.eed.state.ak.us/EarlyDev/
ccresource.html

**Alaska Department of Education and
Early Development**
Attn.: State Director, Child Nutrition Programs
801 West 10th Street, Suite 200
Juneau, AK 99801-1894
Phone: 907-465-3316
Fax: 907-463-5279
http://www.eed.state.ak.us/tls/schoolhealth/
nutrition.html

Alaska Child Support Enforcement Division
550 West 7th Avenue, Suite 312
Anchorage, AK 99501-6699
Phone: 907-269-6804
Fax: 907-269-6868
http://www.csed.state.ak.us

**U.S. Small Business Administration
Alaska District Office**
510 L Street, Suite 310
Anchorage, AK 99501
Phone: 907-271-4022
Fax: 907-271-4545
Toll Free: (outside Anchorage) 1-800-755-7034

To report suspected child abuse in Alaska,
call 1-800-478-4444.

State Home Page: http://www.state.ak.us/

State Child Care Home Page:
http://www.eed.state.ak.us/EarlyDev/

American Samoa

**American Samoa Department of
Human and Social Services
American Samoa**
G.P.O. Box 997534
Pago Pago, AS 96799
Phone: 684-633-2696
Fax: 684-633-7449

Arizona

**Arizona Department of Economic Security
Child Care Administration**
1789 W. Jefferson, 801A
Phoenix, AZ 85007
Phone: 602-542-4248
Fax: 602-542-4197

**Arizona Governor's Division for Children
Head Start–State Collaboration Office**
1700 West Washington, Suite 101-B
Phoenix, AZ 85007
Phone: 602-542-3483
Fax: 602-542-4644
http://www.governor.state.az.us/children/
e_head.html

**Department of Health Services
Office of Child Care Licensure**
1647 East Morten, Suite 230
Phoenix, AZ 85020
Phone: 602-674-4220
Fax: 602-861-0674
http://www.hs.state.az.us/als/childcare/index.html

Department of Economic Security
Child Care Administration, Site Code 801A
P.O. Box 6123
1789 W. Jefferson
Phoenix, AZ 85005
Phone: 602-542-4248
Fax: 602-542-4197

Children and Family Services (Southern Arizona)
2800 East Broadway
Tucson, AZ 85716
Phone: 520-881-8940
http://www.arizonachildcare.org

**Association for Supportive Child Care
(Northern and Central Arizona)**
3910 S. Rural Road, Suite O
Tempe, AZ 85282
Phone: 602-736-5935

**Child Care Resource and Referral State
Administration
DES/Child Care Administration**
P.O. Box 6123, Site Code 801A
Phoenix, AZ 85005
Phone: 602-542-2575

Arizona State Department of Education
Attn.: State Director, Student Services
1535 West Jefferson Avenue, Bin 7
Phoenix, AZ 85007
Phone: 602-542-8700
Fax: 602-542-3818
http://www.ade.state.az.us/health-safety/
cnp/cacfp/

**Arizona Department of Economic Security
Division of Child Support Enforcement**
P.O. Box 40458, Site Code 021A
Phoenix, AZ 85067
Phone: 602-274-7646
Fax: 602-274-8250
http://www.de.state.az.us/links/dcse/index.html

**U.S. Small Business Administration
Arizona District Office**
2828 North Central Avenue, Suite 800
Phoenix, Arizona 85004
Phone: 602-745-7200
Fax: 602-745-7210

To report suspected child abuse in Arizona,
call toll free 1-888-SOS-CHILD (888-767-2445).

State Home Page: http://www.state.az.us/

State Child Care Home Page:
http://www.de.state.az.us/links/chdcare/cca.html

Arkansas

**Arkansas Department of Human Services
Division of Child Care and Early Education**
Donaghey Plaza South MS S140
P.O. Box 1437
Little Rock, AR 72203-1437
Phone: 501-682-4891
Fax: 501-682-4897
http://www.state.ar.us/childcare/

**Arkansas Head Start Association
Head Start–State Collaboration Project**
523 South Louisiana, Suite 301
Little Rock, AR 72201
Phone: 501-371-0740
Fax: 501-370-9109
http://www.arheadstart.org/

**Child Care Licensing
Division of Child Care and
Early Childhood Education**
P.O. Box 1437, Slot 720
Little Rock, AR 72203-1437
Phone: 501-682-8590
Fax: 501-682-2317
http://www.state.ar.us/childcare/provinfo.html

**Arkansas Department of
Human Services
Division of Child Care and
Early Childhood Education**
101 East Capitol, Suite 106
Little Rock, AR 72201
Toll Free: 1-800-445-3316

**Arkansas Department of Human Services
Division of Child Care and
Early Childhood Education**
Attn.: State Director, Special Nutrition
Programs
P.O. Box 1437, Slot 705
Little Rock, AR 72203-1437
Phone: 501-682-8869
Fax: 501-682-2234
http://www.state.ar.us/childcare/usda.html

Arkansas Office of Child Support Enforcement
Department of Finance and Administration
Division of Revenue
712 West 3rd, P.O. Box 8133
Little Rock, AR 72203
Phone: 501-682-6169
Fax: 501-682-6002
http://www.state.ar.us/dfa/childsupport/index.html

U.S. Small Business Administration
Arkansas District Office
2120 Riverfront Drive, Suite 100
Little Rock, AR 72202
Phone: 501-324-5871
Fax: 501-324-5199

To report suspected child abuse in Arkansas,
call 1-800-482-5964.

State Home Page: http://www.state.ar.us/

State Child Care Home Page:
http://www.state.ar.us/childcare/

California

California State Department of Education
Child Development Division
560 J Street, Suite 220
Sacramento, CA 95814-4785
Phone: 916-322-6233
Fax: 916-323-6853
http://www.cde.ca.gov/cyfsbranch/child_development/

California Department of Education
Child Development Division
Head Start–State Collaboration Office
560 J Street, Suite 220
Sacramento, CA 95814
Phone: 916-323-9727
Fax: 916-323-6853
http://www.cde.ca.gov/cyfsbranch/child_development/
CHSSCOview.htm

Department of Social Services
Community Care Licensing Division
744 P Street, Mail Stop 19-50
Sacramento, CA 95814
Phone: 916-324-4031
Fax: 916-323-8352
http://www.ctc.ca.gov/credentialinfo/leaflets/cl797/
cl797.html

California Child Care Resource and
Referral Network
111 New Montgomery Street
San Francisco, CA 94105
Phone: 415-882-0234
Fax: 415-882-6233
http://www.rrnetwork.org/

California Department of Education
Attn.: State Director, Nutrition Services Division
P.O. Box 944272
560 J Street, Room 270
Sacramento, CA 95814-2342
Phone: 916-323-7311
Fax: 916-327-0503
http://www.cde.ca.gov/nsd/ccfp/

California Department of
Child Support Services
744 P Street, Mail Stop 17-29
Sacramento, CA 95814
Phone: 916-654-1556
Fax: 916-653-8690
http://www.childsup.cahwnet.gov/Default.htm

U.S. Small Business Administration
455 Market Street, 6th Floor
San Francisco, CA 94105-2420
Phone: 415-744-6820

To report suspected child abuse in California,
call any state licensing office, any law enforcement
office, or any child protective office in any of the
county social/health/welfare offices.

State Home Page: http://www.state.ca.us/

State Child Care Home Page:
http://www.cde.ca.gov/cyfsbranch/child_development/

Child Development Division's Care about Quality
Web site: http://www.careaboutquality.org

Colorado

Colorado Department of Human Services
Division of Child Care
1575 Sherman Street
Denver, CO 80203-1714
Phone: 303-866-5958
Fax: 303-866-4453

**Colorado Head Start–State
Collaboration Project**
136 State Capitol Building
Denver, CO 80203
Phone: 303-866-4609
Fax: 303-866-6368

**Department of Human Services
Division of Child Care**
1575 Sherman Street, First Floor
Denver, CO 80203-1714
Phone: 303-866-5958
Fax: 303-866-4453
http://www.cdhs.state.co.us/childcare/home.html

**Colorado Office of Resource and
Referral Agencies**
7853 E. Arapahoe Court, Suite 3300
Englewood, CO 80112-1377
Phone: 303-290-9088
Fax: 303-290-8005
http://www.corra.org

**Colorado Department of Public
Health and Environment**
Attn.: State Director
FCHSD-CAC-A4
4300 Cherry Creek Drive South
Denver, CO 80222-1530
Phone: 303-692-2330
Fax: 303-756-9926
http://www.cdphe.state.co.us/fc/fchom.asp#cacfp

**Colorado Department of Human Services
Division of Child Support Enforcement**
1575 Sherman Street, 2nd Floor
Denver, CO 80203-1714
Phone: 303-839-1203
http://www.childsupport.state.co.us/

U.S. Small Business Administration
721 19th Street, Suite 426
Denver, CO 80202-2517
Phone: 303-844-2607
Fax: 303-844-6468

To report suspected child abuse in Colorado,
call any county department of social services.

State Home Page: http://www.state.co.us/

State Child Care Home Page:
http://www.cdhs.state.co.us/childcare

Connecticut

**Connecticut Department of Social Services
Family Services/ Child Care Team**
25 Sigourney Street, 10th Floor
Hartford, CT 06106-5033
Phone: 860-424-5006
Fax: 860-951-2996

**Connecticut Head Start–State
Collaboration Office
Department of Social Services**
25 Sigourney Street
Hartford, CT 06106
Phone: 860-424-5066
Fax: 860-951-2996

**Connecticut Department of Public Health
Child Day Care Licensing**
410 Capitol Avenue
Mail Station 12 DAC
P.O. Box 340308
Hartford, CT 06134-0308
Phone: 860-509-8045
Fax: 860-509-7541
http://www.dph.state.ct.us/BRS/Day_Care/
day_care.htm

**United Way of Connecticut/
Child Care Infoline**
1344 Silas Deane Highway
Rocky Hill, CT 06067
Phone: 860-571-7544
Fax: 860-571-7525
http://www.infoline.org/parents/childcare/default.asp

Connecticut Department of Education
Attn.: State Director, Child Nutrition Programs
25 Industrial Park Road
Middletown, CT 06457-1543
Phone: 860-807-2070
Fax: 860-807-2084

**Connecticut Department of Social Services
Bureau of Child Support Enforcement**
25 Sigourney Street
Hartford, CT 06105-5033
Phone: 860-424-5251
Fax: 860-951-2996
http://www.dss.state.ct.us/csrc/csrc.htm

**U.S. Small Business Administration
Connecticut District Office**
330 Main Street, 2nd Floor
Hartford, CT 06106-1800
Phone: 860-240-4700
Fax: 860-240-4659
TTD: 1-800-877-8845

To report suspected child abuse in Connecticut,
call 1-800-842-2288 (TDD/hearing impaired:
1-800-624-5518).

State Home Page: http://www.state.ct.us/

State Child Care Home Page:
http://www.dss.state.ct.us/ccare/ccare.htm

Washington, DC

**District of Columbia Department
of Human Services
Office of Early Childhood Development
Commission on Social Service**
717 14th Street NW, #730
Washington, DC 20005
Phone: 202-727-1839
Fax: 202-727-8166

**District of Columbia Head Start–State
Collaborative Office**
717 14th Street NW, Suite 730
Washington, DC 20005
Phone: 202-727-1839
Fax: 202-727-9709

**Licensing Regulation Administration
Human Services Facility Division**
614 H Street NW, Suite 1003
Washington, DC 20001
Phone: 202-727-7226
Fax: 202-727-7780

Washington Child Development Council
2121 Decatur Place NW
Washington, DC 20008
Phone: 202-387-0002
Fax: 202-332-2834

District of Columbia Public Schools
Attn.: State Director, Division of Logistical
Support, Food Services
3535 V Street NE
Washington, DC 20018-7000
Phone: 202-576-7400
Fax: 202-576-6835

**Office of Paternity and Child
Support Enforcement**
800 9th Street SW, 2nd Floor
Washington, DC 20024-2480
Phone: 202-645-5330
Fax: 202-645-4123

**U.S. Small Business Administration
Washington District Office**
1110 Vermont Avenue NW, 9th Floor
Washington, D.C. 20005
(202) 606-4000

To report suspected child abuse in District of
Columbia, call 202-576-6762 (Metropolitan
Police Department). To report suspected neglect,
call 202-727-0995 (Department of Human Services).

State Home Page: http://www.washingtondc.gov

State Child Care Home Page:
http://dhs.dc.gov/info/earlychildhood.shtm

Delaware

**Delaware Department of Health and
Social Services
Lewis Building–Herman Holloway Campus**
1901 N. DuPont Highway
P.O. Box 906
New Castle, DE 19720
Phone: 302-577-4880
Fax: 302-577-4405

**Delaware Department of Education
CII Branch/ECEC
Head Start–State Collaboration Office**
Townsend Building
P.O. Box 1402
Dover, DE 19903-1402
Phone: 302-739-4667
Fax: 302-739-2388

Department of Services for Children, Youth, and Families
Office of Child Care Licensing
1825 Faulkland Road
Wilmington, DE 19805
Phone: 302-892-5800
Fax: 302-633-5112

The Family and Workplace Connection
3511 Silverside Road, Suite 100
Wilmington, DE 19810
Phone: 302-479-1679
Fax: 302-479-1693
http://www.familyandworkplace.org/

Delaware Department of
Public Instruction
Attn.: State Director,
School Support Services,
Child Nutrition Programs
Townsend Building
Federal and Lockerman Streets
P.O. Box 1402
Dover, DE 19903-1402
Phone: 302-739-4676
Fax: 302-739-6397

Delaware Department of
Health and Social Services
Division of Child Support Enforcement
1901 N. DuPont Highway, Biggs Building
New Castle, DE 19720
Phone: 302-577-4807
Fax: 302-577-4873
http://www.state.de.us/dhss/dcse/

U.S. Small Business Administration
Delaware District Office
824 N. Market Street
Wilmington, DE 19801-3011
Phone: 302-573-6294
Fax: 302-573-6060

To report suspected child abuse in Delaware, call 1-800-292-9582.

State Home Page: http://www.state.de.us/

State Child Care Home Page:
http://www.state.de.us/dhss/dss/childcare.html

Florida

Florida Partnership for School Readiness
The Holland Building, Room 251
600 S. Calhoun Street
Tallahassee, FL 32399-0001
Phone: 850-488-0337
Fax: 850-922-5188

Florida Partnership for School Readiness
Head Start–State Collaboration Office
The Holland Building, Room 251
600 S. Calhoun Street
Tallahassee, FL 32399
Phone: 850-488-0337
Fax: 850-922-5188

Department of Children and Families
Family Safety and Preservation
Child Care Services
1317 Winewood Boulevard
Building 6, Room 389A
Tallahassee, FL 32399-0700
Phone: 850-488-4900
Fax: 850-488-9584

Florida Children's Forum
2807 Remington Green Circle
Tallahassee, FL 32308
Phone: 850-681-7002
Alt. Phone: 877-FL-CHILD
Fax: 850-681-9816
http://fcforum.org/

Florida Department of Health
Attn.: State Director, Child Food Care Program
2020 Capital Circle SE, Bin A17
Building 5, Room 301
Tallahassee, FL 32399-0700
Phone: 850-488-3875
Fax: 850-414-1622
http://www.doh.state.fl.us/ccfp/

Florida Department of Revenue
Child Support Enforcement Program
P.O. Box 8030
Tallahassee, FL 32314-8030
Phone: 850-488-8733
Fax: 850-488-4401
http://sun6.dms.state.fl.us/dor/childsupport/

U.S. Small Business Administration
South Florida District Office
100 S. Biscayne Boulevard, 7th Floor
Miami, FL 33131
Phone: 305-536-5521
Fax: 305-536-5058

To report suspected child abuse in Florida, call 1-800-96-ABUSE (1-800-962-2873).

State Home Page: http://www.state.fl.us/

State Child Care Home Page:
http://www5.myflorida.com/cf_web/myflorida2/healthhuman/childcare/

Florida Partnership for School Readiness:
http://www.myflorida.com/myflorida/government/governorinitiatives/schoolreadiness/

Georgia

Georgia Department of Human Resources
Child Care and Parent Services Unit
Division of Family and Children Services
Two Peachtree Street NW, Suite 21-293
Atlanta, GA 30303
Phone: 404-657-3438
Fax: 404-657-3489

Georgia Head Start–State Collaboration Office
Georgia Office of School Readiness
10 Park Place South, Suite 200
Atlanta, GA 30303
Phone: 404-656-5957
Fax: 404-651-7184
http://www.osr.state.ga.us/headstart1.html

Department of Human Resources
Office of Regulatory Services,
Child Care Licensing Section
2 Peachtree Street NW
32nd Floor, Room #458
Atlanta, GA 30303-3142
Phone: 404-657-5562
Fax: 404-657-8936
http://www2.state.ga.us/Departments/DHR/ORS/orsccl.htm

Georgia Association of Child Care
Resource and Referral Agencies
P.O. Box 243
Tifton, GA 31793
Phone: 912-382-9919
Fax: 912-382-3749

Georgia Office of School Readiness
Attn.: State Director
10 Park Place South, Suite 200
Atlanta, GA 30303-2927
Phone: 404-651-7431
Fax: 404-651-7429
http://www.osr.state.ga.us/osrhome.html

Georgia Department of Human Resources
Child Support Enforcement
P.O. Box 38450
Atlanta, GA 30334-0450
Phone: 404-657-3851
Fax: 404-657-3326
http://www.cse.dhr.state.ga.us/

U.S. Small Business Administration
Georgia District Office
233 Peachtree Street NE, Suite 1900
Atlanta, GA 30303
Phone: 404-331-0100

To report suspected child abuse in Georgia, call the Division of Family and Children's Services at 404-657-7660.

State Home Page: http://www.state.ga.us/

State Child Care Home Page:
http://www2.state.ga.us/Departments/DHR/ORS/orsccl.htm

Guam

Guam Department of Public Health
and Social Services
Government of Guam
P.O. Box 2816
Agana, GU 96910
Phone: 671-735-7102
Fax: 671-734-5910

U.S. Small Business Administration
Guam Branch Office
400 Route 8, Suite 302
First Hawaiian Bank Building
Mongmong, GU 96927
Phone: 671-472-7419
Fax: 671-472-7365

Hawaii

Hawaii Department of Human Services
Benefit, Employment, and Support
Services Division
820 Mililani Street, Suite 606
Honolulu, HI 96813
Phone: 808-586-7050
Fax: 808-586-5229

Hawaii Department of Education
Community Education Center
Hawaii Head Start–State Collaboration Office
634 Pensacola, Room 99-A
Honolulu, HI 96819
Phone: 808-594-0182
Fax: 808-594-0181

Department of Human Services
Benefit, Employment, and Support
Services Division
820 Mililani Street, Suite 606, Haseko Center
Honolulu, HI 96813
Phone: 808-586-7050
Fax: 808-586-5229

PATCH (People Attentive to Children)
2828 Pa'a Street, Suite 3160
Honolulu, HI 96819
Phone: 808-839-1789
Fax: 808-839-1799
http://www.patch-hi.org/

Hawaii State Department of Education
Attn.: State Director, School Food Services Division
1106 Koko Head Avenue
Honolulu, HI 96816
Phone: 808-733-8400
Fax: 808-732-4293

Hawaii Department of Attorney General
Child Support Enforcement Agency
P.O. Box 1860
Honolulu, HI 96805-1860
Phone: 808-587-3695
Fax: 808-587-3716
http://kumu.icsd.hawaii.gov/csea/csea.htm

U.S. Small Business Administration
Hawaii District Office
300 Ala Moana Boulevard
Room 2-235
Box 50207
Honolulu, HI 96850
Phone: 808-541-2990
Fax: 808-541-2976

To report suspected child abuse in Hawaii, call the appropriate Department of Human Services office:

Oahu: 808-587-5266
Honolulu: 808-622-7111
Wahiawa: 808-959-0669
Maui: 808-242-8418
Kauai: 808-245-3461

State Home Page: http://www.state.hi.us/

State Child Care Home Page: http://www.state.hi.us/dhs

Idaho

Idaho Department of Health and Welfare
Division of Welfare
450 West State Street, 6th Floor
P.O. Box 83720
Boise, ID 83720-0036
Phone: 208-334-5815
Fax: 208-334-5817

Idaho Head Start Association, Inc.
Head Start–State Collaboration Office
200 North 4th Street, Suite 20
Boise, ID 83702
Phone: 208-345-1182
Fax: 208-345-1163
http://www.idahoheadstartassoc.net/

Department of Health and Welfare
Bureau of Family and Children's Services
450 W. State Street
P.O. Box 83720
Boise, ID 83720-0036
Phone: 208-334-5691
Fax: 208-334-6664
http://www2.state.id.us/dhw/hwgd_www/
contentlist.html

Idaho CareLine
Department of Health and Welfare
450 W. State Street, 3rd Floor
P.O. Box 83720
Boise, ID 83720-0036
Toll Free: 1-800-926-2588
TDD: 208-332-7205
http://www2.state.id.us/dhw/hwgd_www/ecic/
CC/Idaho_C8.htm

Idaho Department of Education
Attn.: State Director, Child Nutrition Programs
Len B. Jordan Office Building
650 West State Street
P.O. Box 83720
Boise, ID 83720-0027
Phone: 208-332-6820
Fax: 208-332-6833
http://www.sde.state.id.us/child/

Idaho Department of Health and Welfare
Bureau of Child Support Services
P.O. Box 83720
Boise, ID 83720-0036
Phone: 208-334-5711
Fax: 208-334-0666
http://www2.state.id.us/dhw/childsupport/index.htm

U.S. Small Business Administration
Boise Idaho District Office
1020 Main Street
Boise, ID 83702
Phone: 208-334-1696
Fax: 208-334-9353

To report suspected child abuse in Idaho, call any local department of health and welfare office.

State Home Page: http://www.state.id.us/

State Child Care Home Page:
http://www2.state.id.us/dhw/ecic/home.htm

Illinois

Illinois Department of Human Services
Office of Child Care and Family Services
330 Iles Park Place, Suite 270
Springfield, IL 62718
Phone: 217-785-2559
Fax: 217-524-6029

Illinois Department of Human Services
Head Start–State Collaboration Office
10 Collinsville Avenue, Room 203
East St. Louis, IL 62201
Phone: 618-583-2083
Fax: 618-583-2091

Department of Children and Family Services
Bureau of Licensure and Certification
406 East Monroe Street
Station 60
Springfield, IL 62701-1498
Phone: 217-785-2688
Fax: 217-524-3347
http://www.state.il.us/agency/dhs/childcnp.html

Illinois Network of Child Care Resource and Referral Agencies
207 W. Jefferson Street, Suite 503
Bloomington, IL 61701
Phone: 309-829-5327
Fax: 309-828-1808
http://www.ilchildcare.org

Illinois State Board of Education
Attn.: State Director, Nutrition Programs and Education Services
100 North First Street
Springfield, IL 62777-0001
Phone: 217-782-2491
Fax: 217-524-6124

Illinois Department of Public Aid
Division of Child Support Enforcement
32 W. Randolph Street, Room 923
Chicago, IL 60601
Phone: 217-524-4602
Fax: 217-524-4608
http://www.state.il.us/dpa/html/cs_child_
support_news.htm

U.S. Small Business Administration
Illinois District Office
500 W. Madison Street, Suite 1250
Chicago, IL 60661-2511
Phone: 312-353-4528
Fax: 312-886-5688

To report suspected child abuse in Illinois,
call 1-800-252-2873.

State Home Page: http://www.state.il.us/

State Child Care Home Page:
http://www.state.il.us/agency/dhs/childcnp.html

Indiana

Indiana Family and Social Services Administration
Bureau of Child Development
402 W. Washington Street, W392
Indianapolis, IN 46204
Phone: 317-232-1144
Fax: 317-232-7948

Head Start–State Collaboration Office
402 W. Washington Street, Room W461
Indianapolis, IN 46204
Phone: 317-233-6837
Fax: 317-233-4693

Indiana Family and Social Services Administration
Division of Family and Children
Bureau of Child Development–Licensing Unit
P.O Box 7083
Indianapolis, IN 46207
Phone: 317-232-4468 or 317-232-4469
Fax: 317-232-4436
http://www.carefinderindiana.org/

Indiana Family and Social Services Administration
Division of Family and Children
Bureau of Child Development–Licensing Unit
402 W. Washington Street, Room 386
Indianapolis, IN 46204
Phone: 317-232-4521 or 317-232-1660
Fax: 317-232-4436
http://www.carefinderindiana.org/

Indiana Association for Child Care
Resource and Referral
3901 N. Meridian, Suite 350
Indianapolis, IN 46208
Phone: 317-924-5202
Fax: 317-924-5102

Indiana Department of Education
Attn.: State Director, Division of School and Community
Nutrition Programs
State House, Room 229
Indianapolis, IN 46204-2798
Phone: 317-232-0850
Fax: 317-232-0855

Indiana Child Support Bureau
402 W. Washington Street, Room W360
Indianapolis, IN 46204
Phone: 317-232-4877
Fax: 317-233-4925
http://www.in.gov/fssa/children/support/index.html

U.S. Small Business Administration
Indiana District Office
429 N. Pennsylvania Street, Suite 100
Indianapolis, IN 46204-1873
Phone: 317-226-7272
TTD: 317-226-5338
FAX: 317-226-7264

To report suspected child abuse in Indiana,
call 1-800-562-2407.

State Home Page: http://www.state.in.us/

State Child Care Home Page:
http://www.state.in.us/fssa/children/bcd/

Iowa

Iowa Department of Human Services
Division of ACFS
Hoover State Office Building, 5th Floor
Des Moines, IA 50319-0114
Phone: 515-242-5994
Fax: 515-281-4597

Iowa Department of Education
Bureau of Children, Families, and
Community Services
Head Start–State Collaboration Office
Grimes State Office Building
Des Moines, IA 50319-0146
Phone: 515-242-6024
Fax: 515-242-6019

Department of Human Services
Adult, Children, and Family Services
Child Day Care Unit
Hoover State Office Building, 5th Floor
Des Moines, IA 50319
Phone: 515-281-4357; 515-281-5994
Fax: 515-281-4597

Iowa Child Care and Early Education Network
1021 Fleming Building
218 Sixth Avenue
Des Moines, IA 50309
Phone: 515-883-1206
Fax: 515-244-8997
http://users.dwx.com/icceen/

Iowa Department of Education
Attn.: State Director, Food and Nutrition Bureau
Grimes State Office Building
Des Moines, IA 50319-0146
Phone: 515-281-4757
Fax: 515-281-6548

Iowa Department of Human Services
Economic Assistance, Child Support Recovery Unit
Hoover Building, 5th Floor
Des Moines, IA 50319
Phone: 515-281-5580
Fax: 515-281-8854
http://www.dhs.state.ia.us/boc/boc.asp

U.S. Small Business Administration
Des Moines District
210 Walnut Street, Room 749
Des Moines IA 50309-2186
Phone: 515-284-4422

To report suspected child abuse in Iowa, call 1-800-362-2178.

State Home Page: http://www.state.ia.us/

State Child Care Home Page:
http://www.dhs.state.ia.us/ACFS/ACFS.asp

Kansas

Kansas Department of Social and
Rehabilitation Services
Docking State Office Building, Room 681 W
915 SW Harrison
Topeka, KS 66612
Phone: 785-296-3349
Fax: 785-296-0146
http://www.srkansas.org/

Kansas Department of Social and
Rehabilitation Services
Head Start–State Collaboration Office
Docking State Office Building
915 SW Harrison, Room 651 South
Topeka, KS 66612
Phone: 785-368-6354
Fax: 785-296-0146

Department of Health and Environment
Child Care Licensing and Registration
1000 SW Jackson
Signature State Office Building, Suite 200
Topeka, KS 66612-1274
Phone: 785-296-1270
Fax: 785-296-0803

Kansas Association of Child Care
Resource and Referral Agencies
112 W. Iron
Salina, KS 67401
Phone: 785-823-3343
Fax: 785-823-3385
http://www.kaccrra.org/index.html

Kansas State Board of Education
Attn.: State Director, Nutrition Services
120 East 10th Street
Topeka, KS 66612-1182
Phone: 785-296-2276
Fax: 785-296-1413
http://www.ksbe.state.ks.us/fsims/fsims.html

Kansas Department of Social and
Rehabilitation Services
Child Support Enforcement Program
P.O. Box 497
Topeka, KS 66601
Phone: 913-296-3237
Fax: 913-296-5206
http://www.srkansas.org/services/cse.htm

U.S. Small Business Administration
Kansas District Office
271 W. Third Street North, Suite 2500
Wichita, Kansas 67202-1212
Phone: 316-269-6616
Fax: 316-269-6499

To report suspected child abuse in Kansas,
call 1-800-922-5330.

State Home Page: http://www.accesskansas.org

State Child Care Home Page:
http://www.srskansas.org/ees/child_care.htm

Kentucky

Kentucky Cabinet for Families and Children
Department for Community-Based Services
Division of Child Care
275 East Main Street, 3E-B6
Frankfort, KY 40621
Phone: 502-564-2524
Fax: 502-564-2467

Kentucky Head Start–State Collaboration Office
275 East Main Street, 2W-E
Frankfort, KY 40621
Phone: 502-564-8099
Fax: 502-564-9183
http://www.kih.net/kycollaboration

Cabinet for Health Services
Division of Licensing and Regulation
C.H.R. Building
275 East Main Street, 5E-A
Frankfort, KY 40621
Phone: 502-564-2800
Fax: 502-564-6546

Community Coordinated Child Care (4-C)
1215 South Third Street
Louisville, KY 40203
Phone: 502-636-1358
Fax: 502-636-1488
http://www.4cforkids.org/

Kentucky Cabinet for Human Resources
Division of Child Support Enforcement
275 East Main Street
Frankfort, KY 40621
Phone: 502-564-2285
Fax: 502-564-5988

Kentucky Department of Education
Attn.: State Director, Division of School
and Community Nutrition
500 Mero Street
Frankfort, KY 40601
Phone: 502-573-4390
Fax: 502-573-6775
http://www.kde.state.ky.us/odss/nutrition/
default.asp

U.S. Small Business Administration
Romano Mazzoli Federal Building
Kentucky District Office
600 Dr. MLK Jr. Place
Louisville, KY 40202
Phone: 502-582-5761

To report suspected child abuse in Kentucky,
call 1-800-752-6200.

State Home Page: http://www.state.ky.us/

State Child Care Home Page:
http://cfc.state.ky.us/help/child_care.asp

Louisiana

Louisiana Department of Social Services
Child Care Assistance Program
Office of Family Support, FIND Work/
Child Care Division
P.O. Box 91193
Baton Rouge, LA 70821-9193
Phone: 225-342-9106
Fax: 225-342-9111
http://www.dss.state/la.us/offofs/html/child_
care_assistance.html

Louisiana Head Start–State Collaboration Office
412 Fourth Street, Suite 101
Baton Rouge, LA 70802-5212
Phone: 225-219-4245
Fax: 225-219-4248
http://www.dss.state.la.us/offofs/html/head_
start_collaboration_proje.html

Department of Social Services
Bureau of Licensing
P.O. Box 3078
Baton Rouge, LA 70821
Phone: 504-922-0015
Fax: 504-922-0014
http://www.dss.state.la.us/offofs/html/child_
care_assistance.html

Agenda for Children
1326 Josephine Street
P.O. Box 51837
New Orleans, LA 70151
Phone: 504-586-8509
Fax: 504-586-8522
http://www.agendaforchildren.org/

Louisiana Department of Education
Attn.: State Director, Food and Nutrition Services
655 North Fifth Street
P.O. Box 94064
Baton Rouge, LA 70804-9064
Phone: 504-342-3720
Fax: 504-342-3305

Louisiana Office of Family Support
Support Enforcement Services
P.O. Box 94065
Baton Rouge, LA 70804-4065
Phone: 504-342-4780
Fax: 504-342-7397

U.S. Small Business Administration
Louisiana District Office
365 Canal Street, Suite 2820
New Orleans, LA 70130
Phone: 504-589-6685

To report suspected child abuse in Louisiana, call any local child protective agency.

State Home Page: http://www.state.la.us/

State Child Care Home Page:
http://www.dss.state.la.us/offofs/html/child_
care assistance.html

Maine

Maine Department of Human Services
Office of Child Care and Head Start
11 State House Station
Augusta, ME 04333-0011
Phone: 207-287-5060
Fax: 207-287-5031

Department of Human Services
Office of Child Care and Head Start
Head Start–State Collaboration Office
11 State House Station
Augusta, ME 04333-0011
Phone: 207-287-5060
Fax: 207-287-5031

Bureau of Child and Family Services
221 State Street
Augusta, ME 04333
Phone: 207-287-5060
Fax: 207-287-5031

Child Care Connections
307 Cumberland Avenue
Portland, ME 04104
Phone: 207-775-6503
Fax: 207-775-7327

Maine Department of Human Services
Attn.: State Director, Child and Adult Food Care
Program, Division of Purchased and Support Services
221 State House Station
Augusta, ME 04333
Phone: 207-287-5060
Fax: 207-287-5282

Maine Department of Human Services
Bureau of Income Maintenance
Division of Support Enforcement and Recovery
11 State House Station
Augusta, ME 04333
Phone: 207-287-2866
Fax: 207-287-5096

U.S. Small Business Administration
Maine District Office
40 Western Avenue
Augusta, ME 04330
Phone: 207-622-8274
Fax: 207-622-8277

To report suspected child abuse in Maine,
call 1-800-452-1999.

State Home Page: http://www.state.me.us/

State Child Care Home Page:
http://www.state.me.us/dhs/

Maryland

Maryland Department of Human Resources
Child Care Administration
311 W. Saratoga Street, 1st Floor
Baltimore, MD 21201
Phone: 410-767-7128
Fax: 410-333-8699
http://www.dhr.state.md.us/cca-home.htm

Department of Human Resources
Office of Licensing
Child Care Administration
311 W. Saratoga Street, 1st Floor
Baltimore, MD 21201
Phone: 410-767-7805
Fax: 410-333-8699

Maryland Head Start–State Collaboration Office
Governor's Office for Children,
Youth and Families
301 West Preston Street, 15th Floor
Baltimore, MD 21201
Phone: 410-767-4196
Fax: 410-333-5248
http://www.ocyf.state.md.us/2g.htm

Maryland Committee for Children, Inc.
608 Water Street
Baltimore, MD 21202
Phone: 410-752-7588
Fax: 410-752-6286
http://mdchildcare.org/mdcfc/mcc.html

Maryland State Department of Education
Attn.: State Director, Nutrition and
Transportation Services
200 West Baltimore Street, 3rd Floor
Baltimore, MD 21201-2595
Phone: 410-767-0199
Fax: 410-333-2635
http://www.msde.state.md.us/programs/
foodandnutrition/childfood.html

Maryland Child Support Enforcement Program
311 West Saratoga Street
Baltimore, MD 21201
Phone: 800-332-6347
Fax: 410-333-8992
http://www.dhr.state.md.us/csea/index.htm

U.S. Small Business Administration
Baltimore District Office
City Crescent Building, 6th Floor
10 South Howard Street
Baltimore, MD 21201
Phone: 410-962-4392
Fax: 410-962-1805

To report suspected child abuse in Maryland,
call 1-800-332-6347.

State Home Page: http://www.mec.state.md.us/

State Child Care Home Page:
http://www.dhr.state.md.us/cca-home.htm

Massachusetts

Massachusetts Office of Child Care Services
One Ashburton Place, Room 1105
Boston, MA 02108
Phone: 617-626-2000
Fax: 617-626-2028
http://www.qualitychildcare.org/

Executive Office of Health and Human Services
Head Start–State Collaboration Office
One Ashburton Place, #1109
Boston, MA 02108
Phone: 617-727-7600
Fax: 617-727-1396

Office of Child Care Services Licensing
One Ashburton Place, Room 1105
Boston, MA 02108
Phone: 617-727-8900
Fax: 617-626-2028
http://www.qualitychildcare.org/licensing.shtml

Child Care Resource Center
130 Bishop Allen Drive
Cambridge, MA 02139
Phone: 617-547-1063

Massachusetts Department of Education
Attn.: State Director, Nutrition Programs and Services
350 Main Street
Malden, MA 02351
Phone: 781-388-6479
Fax: 781-388-3399
http://www.doe.mass.edu/cnp/

Massachusetts Department of Revenue
Child Support Enforcement Division
141 Portland Street
Cambridge, MA 02139-1937
Phone: 617-577-7200
Fax: 617-621-4991

U.S. Small Business Administration
Massachusetts District Office
10 Causeway Street, Room 265
Boston, MA 02222-1093
Phone: 617-565-5590
Fax: 617-565-5598

To report suspected child abuse in Massachusetts, call
1-800-792-5200.

State Home Page: http://www.state.ma.us/

State Child Care Home Page:
http://www.qualitychildcare.org/

Michigan

Michigan Family Independence Agency
Child Development and Care Division
235 South Grand Avenue, Suite 1302
P.O. Box 30037
Lansing, MI 48909-7537
Phone: 517-373-0356
Fax: 517-241-7843

Michigan Family Independence Agency
Head Start–State Collaboration Project
235 South Grand Avenue, Suite 1302
P.O. Box 30037
Lansing, MI 48909
Phone: 517-335-3610
Fax: 517-241-9033

Department of Consumer and Industry Services
Division of Child Day Care Licensing
7109 W. Saginaw, 2nd Floor
P.O. Box 30650
Lansing, MI 48909-8150
Phone: 517-373-8300
Fax: 517-335-6121
http://www.cis.state.mi.us/brs/cdc/home.htm

Michigan 4C Association
(Child Care Food Program Agency)
2875 Northwind Drive, #200
East Lansing, MI 48823
Phone: 517-351-4171

Michigan Department of Education
Attn.: State Director, School Management Services
P.O. Box 30008
Lansing, MI 48909
Phone: 517-373-8642
Fax: 517-373-4022
http://www.state.mi.us/mde/off/oss/index.
htm#FoodNutrition

Michigan Department of Social Services
Office of Child Support
P.O. Box 30478
Lansing, MI 48909-7978
Phone: 517-373-7570
Fax: 517-373-4980

U.S. Small Business Administration
Michigan District Office
477 Michigan Avenue, Suite 515,
McNamara Building
Detroit, MI 48226
Phone: 313-226-6075
Fax: 313-226-4769
E-mail: michigan@sba.gov

To report suspected child abuse in Michigan,
call 1-800-942-4357

State Home Page: http://www.state.mi.us/

State Child Care Home Page:
http://www.mfia.state.mi.us/chldDevCare/cdc1.htm

Minnesota

Minnesota Department of Children,
Families, and Learning
1500 Highway 36 West
Roseville, MN 55113-4266
Phone: 651-582-8562
Fax: 651-582-8496
http://www.educ.state.mn.us/

Minnesota Department of Children,
Families, and Learning
Head Start–State Collaboration Office
1500 Highway 36 West
Roseville, MN 55113
Phone: 651-582-8405
Fax: 651-582-8491
http://cfl.state.mn.us/OEO/head_start.htm

Department of Human Services
Division of Licensing
444 Lafayette Road
St. Paul, MN 55155-3842
Phone: 561-296-3971
Fax: 561-297-1490
http://www.dhs.state.mn.us/Licensing/ChildCare/
default.htm

Minnesota CCR&R Network
380 E. Lafayette Road, Suite 103
St. Paul, MN 55107
Phone: 651-290-9704
Fax: 651-290-9785
http://www.mnchildcare.org/

Minnesota Department of Children,
Families, and Learning
Attn.: State Director, Food and Nutrition Services
1500 Highway 36 West
Roseville, MN 55113-4266
Phone: 651-582-8526
Fax: 651-582-8500
http://fns.state.mn.us/

Minnesota Department of Human Services
Office of Child Support Enforcement
444 Lafayette Road, 4th Floor
St. Paul, MN 55155-3846
Phone: 612-297-8232
Fax: 612-297-4450

U.S. Small Business Administration
Minnesota District Office
100 N. Sixth Street, Suite 210-C Butler Square
Minneapolis, Minnesota 55403
Phone: 612-370-2324
Fax: 612-370-2303

To report suspected child abuse in Minnesota,
call 612-296-3971 or any county child
protection director.

State Home Page: http://www.state.mn.us/

State Child Care Home Page:
http://cfl.state.mn.us/ecfi/

Mississippi

Mississippi Department of Human Services
Office for Children and Youth
750 North State Street
Jackson, MS 39202
Phone: 601-359-4544
Fax: 601-359-4422

Mississippi Department of Human Services
Office for Children and Youth
Head Start–State Collaboration Office
750 North State Street
Jackson, MS 39202
Phone: 601-359-4553
Fax: 601-359-4422
http://www.mdhs.state.ms.us/ocy_hsco.html

Department of Health
Division of Child Care
P.O. Box 1700
Jackson, MS 39215-1700
Phone: 601-576-7613
Fax: 601-576-7813

Mississippi Forum on Children and Families
737 North President Street
Jackson, MS 39202
Phone: 601-355-4911
Fax: 601-355-4813
http://www.mfcf.org/

Mississippi Department of Education
Attn.: State Director, Bureau of Child Nutrition
550 High Street, Suite 1601
P.O. Box 771
Jackson, MS 39205-0771
Phone: 601-354-7015
Fax: 601-354-7595

Mississippi Department of Human Services
Division of Child Support Enforcement
P.O. Box 352
Jackson, MS 39205
Phone: 601-359-4863
Fax: 601-359-4415

U.S. Small Business Administration
Mississippi District Office
AmSouth Bank Plaza
210 E. Capitol Street, Suite 900
Jackson, MS 39201
Phone: 601-965-4378
Fax: 601-965-5629 or 601-965-4294

To report suspected child abuse in Mississippi, call 1-800-222-8000.

State Home Page: http://www.state.ms.us

State Child Care Home Page:
http://www.mdhs.state.ms.us/ocy.html

Missouri

Missouri Department of Social Services
Division of Family Services
Income Maintenance
P.O. Box 88
Jefferson City, MO 65103
Phone: 573-751-3221
Fax: 573-751-0507

Missouri Head Start–State Collaboration Office
University of Missouri
31 Stanley Hall
Columbia, MO 65211-6280
Phone: 573-884-0579
Fax: 573-884-0598
http://www.moheadstart.org/

Department of Health
Bureau of Child Care, Safety, and Licensure
1715 Southridge
Jefferson City, MO 65109
Phone: 573-751-2450
Fax: 573-526-5345
http://www.health.state.mo.us/LicensingAnd
Certification/welcome.html

Child Day Care Association
4236 Lindell Boulevard, Suite 300
St. Louis, MO 63108
Phone: 314-351-1412
Alt. Phone: 800-467-CDCA
Fax: 314-531-4184

Missouri Department of Health
Attn.: State Director, Bureau of Food Programs and
Nutrition Education
P.O. Box 570, 930 Wildwood
Jefferson City, MO 65102-0570
Phone: 573-751-6269
Fax: 573-526-3679
http://www.health.state.mo.us/NutritionServices/
EatForHealth.html

Missouri Department of Social Services
Division of Child Support Enforcement
P.O. Box 1527
Jefferson City, MO 65102-1527
Phone: 573-751-1374
Fax: 573-751-8450
http://www.dss.state.mo.us/cse/index.htm

U.S. Small Business Administration
St. Louis District Office
815 Olive Street, Room 242
St. Louis, MO 63101
Phone: 314-539-6600
Fax: 314-539-3785

To report suspected child abuse in Missouri,
call 1-800-392-3738.

State Home Page: http://www.state.mo.us

State Child Care Home Page:
http://www.dss.state.mo.us/dfs/early/index.htm

Montana

Montana Department of Public Health and
Human Services
Human and Community Services Division
Early Childhood Services Bureau
P.O. Box 202952
Helena, MT 59620-2952
Phone: 406-444-1828
Fax: 406-444-2547

Head Start–State Collaboration Office
P.O. Box 202952
Helena, MT 59620-2952
Phone: 406-444-0589
Fax: 406-444-2547

Department of Public Health and
Human Services (DPHHS)
Quality Assurance Division (QAD)
Licensing Bureau
Child Care Licensing Program
P.O. Box 202953
Helena, MT 59620-2953
http://www.dphhs.state.mt.us/divisions/qad/qad.htm

Montana Child Care Resource and Referral Network
c/o Child Care Resources
127 East Main, Suite 314
Missoula, MT 59801
Phone: 406-728-6446
Alt. Phone: 800-728-6446
http://www.childcareresources.org/

Montana Department of Public Health and
Human Services
Attn.: State Director, Children's Services
Cogswell Building, 1400 Broadway
P.O. Box 8005
Helena, MT 59604
Phone: 406-444-1828
Fax: 406-444-5956

Department of Social and Rehabilitation Services
Child Support Enforcement Division
P.O. Box 202943
Helena, MT 59620
Phone: 406-442-7278
Fax: 406-442-1370

U.S. Small Business Administration
Montana District Office
Federal Building
10 West 15th Street, Suite 1100
Helena, MT 59626

To report suspected child abuse in Montana,
call 1-800-332-6100.

State Home Page: http://www.state.mt.us/

State Child Care Home Page:
http://www.dphhs.state.mt.us/divisions/hcs/hcs.htm

Mariana Islands

Northern Mariana Islands State Board of Education
CNMI P.O. Box 1370 CK
Saipan MP 96950
Phone: 670-664-3714
Fax: 670-664-3717

Nebraska

Nebraska Health and Human Services System
Child Care
P.O. Box 95044
Lincoln, NE 68509-5044
Phone: 402-471-9676
Fax: 402-471-7763

Nebraska Head Start–State Collaboration Office
Nebraska Department of Education, Office of
Children and Families
301 Centennial Mall South
P.O. Box 94987
Lincoln, NE 68509-4987
Phone: 402-471-3501
Fax: 402-471-0117
http://www.nde.state.ne.us/ECH/HeadStart/
HSSCP.html

Nebraska Department of Health and
Human Services
Child Care
P.O. Box 95044
Lincoln, NE 68509-5044
Phone: 402-471-7763
Fax: 402-471-9455
http://www.hhs.state.ne.us/crl/childcare.htm

Midwest Child Care Association
5015 Dodge Street
Omaha, NE 68132
Phone: 402-558-6794

Nebraska Department of Education
Attn.: State Director, Child Nutrition Programs
301 Centennial Mall South
Lincoln, NE 68509-4987
Phone: 402-471-3566
Fax: 402-471-4407
http://www.nde.state.ne.us/NS/index.htm

Nebraska Department of Health and
Human Services
Child Support Enforcement Office
P.O. Box 94728
Lincoln, NE 68509-4728
Phone: 402-479-5555
Fax: 402-479-5145
http://www.hhs.state.ne.us/cse/cseindex.htm

U.S. Small Business Administration
11145 Mill Valley Road
Omaha, NE 68154
Phone: 402-221-4691
Fax: 402-221-3680

To report suspected child abuse in Nebraska,
call 1-800-652-1999.

State Home Page: http://www.state.ne.us/

State Child Care Home Page:
http://www.hhs.state.ne.us/chc/chcindex.htm

Nevada

Nevada Department of Human Resources
Welfare Division
1470 E. College Parkway
Carson City, NV 89706
Phone: 775-684-0500
Fax: 775-684-0617
http://www.welfare.state.nv.us/welfare.htm

Nevada Head Start–State Collaboration Office
Nevada Department of Human Resources,
Community Connections
3987 South McCarran Boulevard
Reno, NV 89502
Phone: 702-688-2284 x227
Fax: 702-688-2558
http://www.nvcommunityconnections.com/programs/
programs.php?programid=1

Department of Human Resources
Division of Child and Family Services
Bureau of Child Care Licensing
3920 E. Idaho Street
Elko, NV 89801
Phone: 775-753-1237
Fax: 775-753-2111

Nevada Department of Education
Attn.: State Director, Health and Safety Programs
700 East Fifth Street
Carson City, NV 89701-5096
Phone: 702-687-9154
Fax: 702-687-9199

Nevada State Welfare Division
Child Support Enforcement Program
2527 N. Carson Street, Capitol Complex
Carson City, NV 89710
Phone: 702-687-4744
Fax: 702-684-8026

U.S. Small Business Administration
Nevada District Office
300 Las Vegas Boulevard South, Suite 1100
Las Vegas, NV 89101
Phone: 702-388-6611
Fax: 702-388-6469

To report suspected child abuse in Nevada,
call 1-800-992-5757.

State Home Page: http://www.state.nv.us/

State Child Care Home Page:
http://www.welfare.state.nv.us

New Hampshire

New Hampshire Department of
Health and Human Services
Division for Children, Youth and Families
Bureau of Child Development
129 Pleasant Street
Concord, NH 03301-3857
Phone: 603-271-8153
Fax: 603-271-7982

New Hampshire Head Start–State
Collaboration Office
New Hampshire Department of
Health and Human Services
Child Development Bureau
129 Pleasant Street
Concord, NH 03301-6505
Phone: 603-271-4454
Fax: 603-271-7982

New Hampshire Department of
Health and Human Services
Office of Program Support
Bureau of Child Care Licensing
129 Pleasant Street
Concord, NH 03301
Phone: 603-271-4624
Fax: 603-271-4782

FamilyWorks/Child and Family Services
500 Amherst Street
Nashua, NH 03063
Phone: 603-889-7189
Fax: 603-889-7104

New Hampshire Department of Education
Attn.: State Director, Nutrition Programs and Services
Bureau
101 Pleasant Street
Concord, NH 03301
Phone: 603-271-3860
Fax: 603-271-1953

Health and Human Services Building
Office of Program Support, Office of Child Support
6 Hazen Drive
Concord, NH 03301
Phone: 603-271-4287
Fax: 603-271-4787

U.S. Small Business Administration
143 N. Main Street
Concord, NH 03301
Phone: 603-225-1400
Fax: 603-225-1409

To report suspected child abuse in New Hampshire,
call 1-800-894-5533.

State Home Page: http://www.state.nh.us/

State Child Care Home Page:
http://www.dhhs.state.nh.us/

New Hampshire Child Care Association:
http://www.nhcca.com

New Jersey

New Jersey Department of Human Services
Division of Family Development
P.O. Box 716
Trenton, NJ 08625
Phone: 609-588-2163
Fax: 609-588-3051

New Jersey Department of Human Services
P.O. Box 700
Trenton, NJ 08625-0700
Phone: 609-984-5321
Fax: 609-292-1903
http://www.state.nj.us/humanservices

Division of Youth and Family Services
Bureau of Licensing
P.O. Box 717
Trenton, NJ 08625-0717
Phone: 609-292-1018
Fax: 609-292-6976

MARO, USDA, FNS, SNP
Attn.: Regional Director
Mercer Corporate Park
300 Corporate Boulevard
Robbinsville, NJ 08691-1598
Phone: 609-259-5050
Fax: 609-259-5128

NJACCRRA
c/o Office for Children
21 Main Street, #114
Hackensack, NJ 07601
Phone: 201-646-3694

New Jersey State Department of Agriculture
Attn.: State Director, Bureau of Child Nutrition
Programs
33 West State Street, 4th Floor
P.O. Box 334
Trenton, NJ 08625-0334
Phone: 609-984-0692
Fax: 609-984-0878

New Jersey Department of Human Services
Division of Family Development
Bureau of Child Support and Paternity Programs
CN 716
Trenton, NJ 08625-0716
Phone: 609-588-2402
Fax: 609-588-3369

U.S. Small Business Administration
New Jersey District Office
Two Gateway Center, 15th Floor
Newark, New Jersey 07102
Phone: 973-645-2434

To report suspected child abuse in New Jersey,
call 1-800-792-8610 (TDD/hearing impaired:
1-800-835-5510).

State Home Page: http://www.state.nj.us/
State Child Care Home Page:
http://www.state.nj.us/humanservices/dfd/chldca.html

New Mexico

New Mexico Department of Children,
Youth, and Families
Child Care Services Bureau
P.O. Drawer 5160, PERA Building, Room 111
Santa Fe, NM 87502-5160
Phone: 505-827-9932
Fax: 505-827-7361

New Mexico Department of Children,
Youth, and Families
Head Start–State Collaboration Office
P.O. Drawer 5160, Room 111
Santa Fe, NM 87502-5160
Phone: 505-827-9952
Fax: 505-827-7361

Child Services Unit / Licensing
PERA Building, Room 111
P.O. Drawer 5160
Santa Fe, NM 87502-5160
Phone: 505-827-4185
Fax: 505-827-7361

YWCA/Carino CCR&R
303 San Mateo Blvd., NE #201
Albuquerque, NM 87108
Phone: 505-265-8565
Alt. Phone: 505-265-8500
Fax: 505-265-8501

New Mexico Children, Youth, and
Families Department
Attn.: State Director, Family Nutrition Bureau
1422 Paseo De Peralta, Building 2
P.O. Box 5160
Santa Fe, NM 87502-5160
Phone: 505-827-9961
Fax: 505-827-9957

New Mexico Human Services Department
Child Support Enforcement Bureau
P.O. Box 25109
Santa Fe, NM 73512
Phone: 505-827-7200
Fax: 505-827-7285

U.S. Small Business Administration
Albuquerque, New Mexico District Office
625 Silver SW, Suite 320
Albuquerque, NM 87102
Phone: 505-346-7909
Fax: 505-346-6711

To report suspected child abuse in New Mexico,
call 1-800-797-3260.

State Home Page: http://www.state.nm.us/

State Child Care Home Page:
http://www.newmexicokids.org/

New York

New York State Department of Family Assistance
Office of Children and Family Services
Bureau of Early Childhood Services
40 North Pearl Street, 11B
Albany, NY 12243
Phone: 518-474-9324
Fax: 518-474-9617

New York State Council on Children and Families
Head Start–State Collaboration Office
5 Empire State Plaza, Suite 2810
Albany, NY 12223-1553
Phone: 518-474-6294
Fax: 518-473-2570
http://capital.net/com/council/headstart.html

New York State Department of Family Assistance
Office of Children and Family Services
Bureau of Early Childhood Services
52 Washington Street, 3N
Rensselaer, NY 12144
Phone: 518-474-9454
Fax: 518-474-9617
http://www.ocfs.state.ny.us/main/becs/default.htm

New York State Child Care Coordinating Council
(Child Care Food Program Agency)
130 Ontario Street
Albany, NY 12206
Phone: 518-463-8663

New York State Department of Health
Attn.: Director
DON-CACFP
Riverview Center
150 Broadway, FL6 West
Albany, NY 12204-2719
Phone: 518-402-7400
Fax: 518-402-7252

New York Department of Social Services
Office of Child Support Enforcement
P.O. Box 14
Albany, NY 12260-0014
Phone: 518-474-9081
Fax: 518-486-3127

For callers from the five boroughs of New York City:
Manhattan, Queens, Brooklyn, Bronx, and Staten Island

New York City Department of Health
Bureau of Day Care
2 Lafayette Street, 22nd Floor
New York, NY 10007
Phone: 212-676-2444 (212-280-9251 for family child
care registration only)
Fax: 212-676-2424
http://www.nyc.gov/html/doh/html/dc/dc.html

U.S. Small Business Administration
26 Federal Plaza, Suite 3100
New York, NY 10278
Phone: 212-264-2454
Fax: 212-264-7751

To report suspected child abuse in New York,
call 1-800-342-3720.

State Home Page: http://www.state.ny.us

State Child Care Home Page:
http://www.ocfs.state.ny.us/main/becs/default.htm

North Carolina

North Carolina Department of
Health and Human Services
Division of Child Development
P.O. Box 29553
Raleigh, NC 27626-0553
Phone: 919-662-4543
Fax: 919-662-4568
http://www.dhhs.state.nc.us/dcd/

North Carolina Head Start–State Collaboration Office
2201 Mail Service Center
Raleigh, NC 27626-2201
Phone: 919-662-4543
Fax: 919-662-4568
http://www.dhhs.state.nc.us/dcd/whatwedo.htm#HS

Division of Child Development Regulatory Services Section
2201 Mail Service Center
Raleigh, NC 27626-2201
Phone: 919-662-4499 or 919-662-4527 or 800-859-0829 (in-state calls only)
Fax: 919-661-4845
http://www.dhhs.state.nc.us/dcd/provider.htm

North Carolina Child Care Resource and Referral Network
460 Bayberry Drive
Chapel Hill, NC 27514
Phone: 919-933-5090
Fax: 919-933-0450

North Carolina Health and Human Services Section
Attn.: State Director, Nutrition Services Section
1330 St. Mary's Street
P.O. Box 10008
Raleigh, NC 27608
Phone: 919-715-0636
Fax: 919-733-1384

North Carolina Department of Human Resources Division of Social Services Child Support Enforcement Section
100 East Six Forks Road
Raleigh, NC 27609-7750
Phone: 919-420-7982
Fax: 919-571-4126

U.S. Small Business Administration North Carolina District Office
200 N. College Street, Suite A2015
Charlotte, NC 28202
Phone: 704-344-6563
Fax: 704-344-6769

To report suspected child abuse in North Carolina, call CARE-LINE: 1-800-662-7030.

State Home Page: http://www.ncgov.com/

State Child Care Home Page:
http://www.dhhs.state.nc.us/dcd/index.htm

North Dakota

North Dakota Department of Human Services Office of Economic Assistance State Capitol Judicial Wing
600 East Boulevard
Bismarck, ND 58505-0250
Phone: 701-328-4603
Fax: 701-328-2359

North Dakota Department of Human Services Head Start–State Collaboration Office
600 East Boulevard
Bismarck, ND 58505
Phone: 701-328-1711
Fax: 701-328-3538
http://www.headstartnd.com/

Department of Human Services Early Childhood Services
600 East Boulevard
State Capitol Building
Bismarck, ND 58505-0250
Phone: 701-328-4809
Fax: 701-328-3538

Lutheran Social Service of North Dakota
615 S. Broadway, Suite L3
Minot, ND 58701-4473
Phone: 701-838-7800
Alt. Phone: 1-800-450-7801
http://www.lssnd.org/program08.html

North Dakota Department of Public Instruction
Attn.: State Director, Child Nutrition and Food Distribution
600 East Boulevard
State Capitol
Bismarck, ND 58505-0440
Phone: 701-328-2294
Fax: 701-328-2461
http://www.dpi.state.nd.us/dpi/child/index.htm

North Dakota Department of Human Services
Child Support Enforcement Agency
P.O. Box 7190
Bismarck, ND 58507-7190
Phone: 701-328-3582
Fax: 701-328-6575

U.S. Small Business Administration
North Dakota District Office
657 Second Avenue North, Room 219
P.O. Box 3086
Fargo, ND 58108
Phone: 701-239-5131
TDD: 701-239-5657
Fax: 701-239-5645
E-mail: north.dakota@sba.gov

To report suspected child abuse in North Dakota, call 1-800-245-3736.

State Home Page: http://www.state.nd.us/

State Child Care Home Page:
http://lnotes.state.nd.us/dhs/dhsweb.nsf/
ServicePages/ChildrenandFamilyServices

Ohio

Ohio Department of Human Services
Bureau of Child Care Services
65 E. State Street, 5th Floor
Columbus, OH 43215
Phone: 614-466-1043
Fax: 614-728-6803

Ohio Head Start–State Collaboration Office
Ohio Family and Children First
Office of the Governor
17 South High Street, Suite 550
Columbus, OH 43215
Phone: 614-752-4044
Fax: 614-728-9441
http://www.ohiofcf.org/

Ohio Department of Job and Family Services
Bureau of Child Care and Development
255 East Main Street, 3rd Floor
Columbus, OH 43215-5222
Phone: 614-466-1043
Fax: 614-728-6803
http://www.state.oh.us/odhs/cdc/index.htm

Ohio Child Care Resource and Referral Association
c/o Action for Children
78 Jefferson Avenue
Columbus, OH 43215
Phone: 614-224-0222
Fax: 614-224-5437
http://www.occrra.org/

Ohio Department of Education
Attn.: State Director, School Food Services Division
65 South Front Street, Room 713
Columbus, OH 43215-4183
Phone: 614-466-2945
Fax: 614-752-7613
http://cns.ode.state.oh.us/

Ohio Department of Human Services
Office of Child Support Enforcement
30 East Broad Street, 31st Floor
Columbus, OH 43266-0423
Phone: 614-752-6561
Fax: 614-752-9760

U.S. Small Business Administration
1111 Superior Avenue
Cleveland, OH 44114-2507
Phone: 216-522-4180
Fax: 216-522-2038

To report suspected child abuse in Ohio, call any county Children's Services Board or the county Human Services Department. Contact district offices of the Human Services Department in Columbus, Cleveland, Cincinnati, Canton, or Toledo for appropriate referral.

State Home Page: http://www.state.oh.us/

State Child Care Home Page:
http://www.state.oh.us/odhs/cdc/index.htm

Oklahoma

Oklahoma Department of Human Services
Division of Child Care
Sequoyah Memorial Office Building
P.O. Box 25352
Oklahoma City, OK 73125-0352
Phone: 405-521-3561
Fax: 405-522-2564

Head Start–State Collaboration Office
Oklahoma Association of Community Action
Agencies (OACAA)
2915 Classen, Suite 215
Oklahoma City, OK 73106
Phone: 405-524-4124
Fax: 405-524-0863
http://www.okacaa.org/headstart/state.html

Department of Human Services
Office of Child Care
P.O. Box 25352
Oklahoma City, OK 73125
Phone: 405-521-3561
Fax: 405-522-2564
http://okdhs.org/childcare/ProviderInfo/provinfo_
licensing.htm

Child Care Resource Center
18 North Norwood
Tulsa, OK 74115
Phone: 918-834-2273
Fax: 918-834-9339
http://www.ccrctulsa.org/

Oklahoma Department of Education
Attn.: State Director, Child Nutrition Section
2500 North Lincoln Boulevard, Room 310
Oklahoma City, OK 73105-4599
Phone: 405-521-3327
Fax: 405-521-2239
http://sde.state.ok.us/pro/nut.html

Oklahoma Department of Human Services
Child Support Enforcement Division
P.O. Box 53552
Oklahoma City, OK 73152
Phone: 405-522-5871
Fax: 405-522-2753

U.S. Small Business Administration
210 Park Avenue, Suite 1300
Oklahoma City, OK 73102
Phone: 405-231-5521
Fax: 405-231-4876

To report suspected child abuse in Oklahoma,
call 1-800-522-3511.

State Home Page: http://www.state.ok.us/

State Child Care Home Page:
http://okdhs.org/childcare/

Oregon

Oregon Department of Employment
Child Care Division
875 Union Street NE
Salem, OR 97311
Phone: 503-947-1400
Fax: 503-947-1428

Oregon Department of Education
Head Start Collaboration Office
Public Service Building
255 Capitol Street NE
Salem, OR 97310-0203
Phone: 503-378-5585 x 662
Fax: 503-373-7968
http://www.ode.state.or.us/stusvc/earlychild/

Employment Department
Child Care Division
875 Union Street NE
Salem, OR 97311
Phone: 503-947-1400
Fax: 503-947-1428
http://findit.emp.state.or.us/childcare/rules.cfm

Oregon Child Care Resource and Referral Network
1828 23rd Street SE
Salem, OR 97302
Phone: 503-375-2644
Fax: 503-399-9858
http://www.open.org/occrrn/

Oregon Department of Education
Attn.: State Director, Child Nutrition and Food
Distribution
Public Services Building
255 Capitol Street NE
Salem, OR 97310-0203
Phone: 503-378-3579
Fax: 503-378-5258
http://www.ode.state.or.us/stusvc/Nutrition/

**Oregon Department of Human Resources
Children, Adults and Family Services
Oregon Child Support Program**
500 Summer Street NE
Salem, OR 97310-1013
Phone: 503-945-5600
Fax: 503-373-7032
http://www.afs.hr.state.or.us/childsupp.html

U.S. Small Business Administration
1515 SW 5th Avenue, Suite 1050
Portland, OR 97201-5494
Phone: 503-326-2682
Fax: 503-326-2808

To report suspected child abuse in Oregon,
call 1-800-854-3508.

State Home Page: http://www.state.or.us/

State Child Care Home Page:
http://findit.emp.state.or.us/childcare/

Pennsylvania

**Pennsylvania Department of Public Welfare
Office of Children, Youth, and Families**
Box 2675
Harrisburg, PA 17105-2675
Phone: 717-783-3856
Fax: 717-787-1529
http://www.dpw.state.pa.us/ocyf/dpwocyf.asp

**Pennsylvania Head Start–State Collaboration Office
Center for Schools and Communities**
1300 Market Street, Suite 12
Lemoyne, PA 17043
Phone: 717-763-1661
Fax: 717-763-2083
http://www.center-school.org/comm_fam/hsscp/
index.html

**Department of Public Welfare,
Bureau of Child Day Care
Office of Children, Youth, and Families**
Bertolino Building, 4th Floor
P.O. Box 2675
Harrisburg, PA 17105-2675
Phone: 717-787-8691
Fax: 717-787-1529
http://www.dpw.state.pa.us/ocyf/childcarewks/
ccwreqccp.asp

Pennsylvania Department of Education
Attn.: State Director, Division of Food and Nutrition
333 Market Street, 4th Floor
Harrisburg, PA 17126-0333
Phone: 717-787-7698
Fax: 717-783-6566
http://www.pde.psu.edu/nutrition/adult.html

**Pennsylvania Department of Public Welfare
Bureau of Child Support Enforcement**
P.O. Box 8018
Harrisburg, PA 17105
Phone: 717-783-5441
Fax: 717-772-4936

U.S. Small Business Administration
900 Market Street, 5th Floor
Philadelphia, PA 19107
Phone: 215-580-2722
Fax: 215-580-2762

To report suspected child abuse in Pennsylvania,
call 1-800-932-0313.

State Home Page: http://www.state.pa.us/

State Child Care Home Page:
http://www.dpw.state.pa.us/ocyf/ocyfdc.asp

Puerto Rico

**Puerto Rico Department of the Family
Administration for Families and Children,
Child Care and Development Program**
Avenida Ponce de Leon, PDA.2, San Juan
Apartado 15091
San Juan, PR 00902-5091
Phone: 787-722-8157
Fax: 787-721-6366

**Puerto Rico Head Start–State
Collaboration Office
Governor's Office
La Fortaleza**
P.O. Box 902-0082
San Juan, PR 00902-0082
Phone: 787-721-7000
Fax: 787-721-5336

Department of Family
Licensing Office
P.O. Box 11398
Santurce, PR 00910
Phone: 787-724-0772
Fax: 787-724-0767

Puerto Rico Department of Education
Attn.: State Director, Food and Nutrition Services
Teniente Cesar Gonzalez
P.O. Box 190759
San Juan, PR 00919-0759
Phone: 787-754-0790
Fax: 787-753-8155

Puerto Rico Department of Social Services
Administration for Child Support
P.O. Box 3349
San Juan, PR 00902
Phone: 787-767-1886
Fax: 787-282-8324

U.S. Small Business Administration
Puerto Rico and Virgin Islands District Office
252 Ponce De Leon Avenue, Suite 201
Hato Rey, PR 00918
Phone: 787-766-5572
Fax: 787-766-5309

To report suspected child abuse in Puerto Rico, call
787-724-7474 (Office of Family Administration).

State Home Page: http://fortaleza.govpr.org

State Child Care Home Page:
http://fortaleza.govpr.org/gobierno/familia1.htm

Rhode Island

Rhode Island Department of Human Services
Louis Pasteur Building, #57
600 New London Avenue
Cranston, RI 02920
Phone: 401-462-3415
Fax: 401-462-6878

Rhode Island Head Start–State
Collaboration Office
Department of Human Services
600 New London Avenue
Cranston, RI 02920
Phone: 401-462-3071
Fax: 401-462-6878

Rhode Island Department of Children,
Youth, and Families
Day Care Licensing Unit
101 Friendship Street
Providence, RI 02903
Phone: 401-528-3624
Fax: 401-528-3650
http://www.dcyf.state.ri.us/licensing.htm

Options for Working Parents
30 Exchange Terrace
Providence, RI 02903
Phone: 401-272-7510
Fax: 401-751-2434

Rhode Island Department of Education
Attn.: State Director, Office of
Integrated Social Services
Shepard Building
255 Westminster Street, Room 600
Providence, RI 02903-3400
Phone: 401-222-4600
Fax: 401-222-4979

Rhode Island Department of Administration
Division of Taxation–Child Support Enforcement
77 Dorrance Street
Providence, RI 09203
Phone: 401-222-2847
Fax: 401-222-2887

U.S. Small Business Administration
380 Westminster Street
Providence, RI 02903
Phone: 401-528-4561
Fax: 401-528-4539

To report suspected child abuse in Rhode Island,
call 1-800-RI-CHILD (1-800-742-4453).

State Home Page: http://www.state.ri.us/

State Child Care Home Page:
http://www.dhs.state.ri.us/

South Carolina

**South Carolina Department of
Health and Human Services
Bureau of Community Services,
Child Care and Development Services**
P.O. Box 8206
1801 Main Street, 8th Floor
Columbia, SC 29202-8206
Phone: 803-898-2570
Fax: 803-898-4510

**South Carolina Department of
Health and Human Services
South Carolina Head Start–State
Collaboration Office**
1801 Main Street, 10th Floor
Columbia, SC 29201
Phone: 803-898-2556
Fax: 803-253-4513

**Department of Social Services
Division of Child Day Care Licensing**
P.O. Box 1520
Room 520
Columbia, SC 29202-1520
Phone: 803-898-7345
Fax: 803-898-7179
http://www.state.sc.us/dss/cdclrs/index.html

**South Carolina Child Care Resources
Interfaith Community Services**
P.O. Box 11570
Columbia, SC 29211-1570
Phone: 803-252-8391
Fax: 803-799-1572

South Carolina Department of Social Services
Attn.: State Director, Food Services Operations
1535 Confederate Avenue, Room 601
P.O. Box 1520
Columbia, SC 29201-1520
Phone: 803-734-9500
Fax: 803-734-9515

**South Carolina Department of Social Services
Child Support Enforcement Division**
P.O. Box 1469
Columbia, SC 29202-1469
Phone: 803-737-5870
Fax: 803-737-6032

U.S. Small Business Administration
1835 Assembly Street, Room 358
Columbia, SC 29201
Phone: 803-765-5377
Fax: 803-765-5962

To report suspected child abuse in South Carolina,
call the Regional Office of the Department of Social
Services.

State Home Page: http://www.myscgov.com/

State Child Care Home Page:
http://www.dhhs.state.sc.us/FAQ/child_care.htm

South Dakota

**South Dakota Department of Social Services
Child Care Services**
700 Governors Drive
Pierre, SD 57501-2291
Phone: 605-773-4766
Fax: 605-773-6834

**South Dakota Department of
Education and Cultural Affairs
Head Start–State Collaboration Office**
700 Governors Drive
Pierre, SD 57501-2291
Phone: 605-773-4640
Fax: 605-773-6846
http://www.state.sd.us/deca/DESR/Childhood/
headstart.htm

**Department of Social Services
Child Care Services
Kneip Building**
700 Governors Drive
Pierre, SD 57501-2291
Phone: 605-773-4766
Fax: 605-773-7294
http://www.state.sd.us/social/CCS/Licensing%
20&%20Registration/licensing2.htm

**South Dakota State University (SDSU)
Family Resource Network**
Box 2218-HDCFS/SDSU
Brookings, SD 57007
Phone: 605-688-5730

tment of
...ural Affairs
...ctor, Child and Adult Nutrition

Governors Drive
Pierre, SD 57501-2291
Phone: 605-773-3413
Fax: 605-773-6846
http://www.state.sd.us/deca/compser/chn.htm

South Dakota Department of Social Services
Office of Child Support Enforcement
700 Governors Drive
Pierre, SD 57501-2291
Phone: 605-773-3641
Fax: 605-773-6834
http://www.state.sd.us/social/cse/index.htm

U.S. Small Business Administration
110 South Phillips Avenue
Sioux Falls, SD 57102
Phone: 605-330-4231
Fax: 605-330-4215

To report suspected child abuse in South Dakota, call the local Department of Social Services office or a local law enforcement agency.

State Home Page: http://www.state.sd.us/

State Child Care Home Page:
http://www.state.sd.us/state/executive/social/
CCS/CCShome.htm

Tennessee

Tennessee Department of Human Services
Child Care Services
Citizens Plaza, 14th Floor
400 Deaderick Street
Nashville, TN 37248-9600
Phone: 615-313-4778
Fax: 615-532-9956

Tennessee Department of Education,
Office of School-Based Support Services
Head Start–State Collaboration Office
Andrew Johnson Tower
710 James Robertson Parkway
Nashville, TN 37243-0375
Phone: 615-741-4849
Fax: 615-532-4899

Department of Human Services
Child Care Services Unit
Citizens Plaza
400 Deaderick Street
Nashville, TN 37248-9800
Phone: 615-313-4778
Fax: 615-532-9956

Tennessee Department of Human Services
Child Care Resource and Referral Center
400 Deaderick Street, 14th Floor
Nashville, TN 37248-9810
Phone: 615-313-4820

Tennessee Department of Human Services
Attn.: State Director, Adult and Community Programs
Citizens Plaza Building, 15th Floor
400 Deaderick Street
Nashville, TN 37248-9500
Phone: 615-313-4749
Fax: 615-532-9956

Tennessee Department of Human Services
Child Support Services
Citizens Plaza Building, 12th Floor
400 Deaderick Street
Nashville, TN 37248-7400
Phone: 615-313-4879
Fax: 615-741-4165

U.S. Small Business Administration
50 Vantage Way, Suite 201
Nashville, TN 37228-1500
Phone: 615-736-5881
Fax: 615-736-7232

To report suspected child abuse in Tennessee, call any county's 24-hour hotline.

State Home Page: http://www.state.tn.us/

State Child Care Home Page:
http://www.state.tn.us/humanserv/childcare.htm

Texas

Texas Workforce Commission
101 East 15th Street, Suite 434T
Austin, TX 78778-0001
Phone: 512-936-3141
Fax: 512-936-3223
http://www.twc.state.tx.us/svcs/childcare/ccinfo.html

Texas Head Start–State Collaboration Office
Office of the Governor
P.O. Box 12428
Austin, TX 78711
Phone: 512-936-4059
Fax: 512-463-7392
http://www.governor.state.tx.us/the_office/
head_start/main.htm

Department of Protective and Regulatory Services
Child Care Licensing
P.O. Box 149030
M.C. E-550
Austin, TX 78714-9030
Toll Free: 800-862-5252 or 512-438-3267
Fax: 512-438-3848
http://www.tdprs.state.tx.us/Child_Care/

Texas Association of Child Care
Resource and Referral Agencies
1500 W. University Avenue, Suite 105
Georgetown, TX 78628
Phone: 512-868-0552
Fax: 512-868-5743
http://www.taccrra.org

Texas Department of Human Services
Attn.: State Director, Client Self-Support Services
1106 Clayton Lane, Suite 217E
P.O. Box 149030
Austin, TX 78714-9030
Phone: 512-483-3941
Fax: 512-467-5855
http://www.dhs.state.tx.us/programs/snp/index.html

Texas Office of the Attorney General
Child Support Division
P.O. Box 12017
Austin, TX 78711-2017
Phone: 512-460-6000
Fax: 512-460-6028
http://www.oag.state.tx.us/child/mainchil.htm

U.S. Small Business Administration
4300 Amon Carter Boulevard, Suite 108
Dallas/Ft.Worth, TX 76155
Phone: 817-684-6581
Fax: 817-684-6588

To report suspected child abuse in Texas,
call 1-800-252-5400.

State Home Page: http://www.state.tx.us/

State Child Care Home Page:
http://www.twc.state.tx.us/svcs/childcare/ccinfo.html

Utah

Utah Department of Workforce Services
Policy and Program Unit
1385 S. State Street
Salt Lake City, UT 84115
Phone: 801-468-0123
Fax: 801-468-0160

Utah Department of Health
Child, Adolescent, and School
Health Programs (CASH)
Head Start–State Collaboration Office
P.O. Box 142001
Salt Lake City, UT 84114-2001
Phone: 801-538-9312
Fax: 801-538-9409
http://www.hlunix.hl.state.ut.us/cfhs/mch/cash/
headstart.html

Department of Health
Bureau of Licensing
Child Care Unit
P.O. Box 142003
Salt Lake City, UT 84114-2003
Phone: 801-538-9299
Fax: 801-538-9259
http://www.health.state.ut.us/hsi/hfl/index.html

Family Connections Resource and Referral Center
Utah Valley State College
800 West 1200 South
Orem, UT 84058
Phone: 801-222-8220

ams

ervices
ervices

⌐

JT 84145-0011
.-536-8911
JI-536-8509

U.S. Small Business Administration
125 South State Street, Room 2231
Salt Lake City, Utah 84138
Phone: 801-524-3209
Fax: 801-524-4160 or 4410

To report suspected child abuse in Utah,
call 801-538-4377 (not toll free).

State Home Page: http://www.state.ut.us/

State Child Care Home Page:
http://occ.dws.state.ut.us/

Vermont

**Vermont Department of Social and
Rehabilitation Services
Agency for Human Services
Child Care Services Division**
103 South Main Street, 2nd Floor
Waterbury, VT 05671-2401
Phone: 802-241-3110
Fax: 802-241-1220
http://www.state.vt.us/srs/childcare/index.htm

**Vermont Head Start–State Collaboration Office
Agency of Human Services**
103 South Main Street
Waterbury, VT 05671-0204
Phone: 802-241-2705
Fax: 802-241-2979

**Department of Social Rehabilitation Services
Child Care Services Division
Child Care Licensing Unit**
103 South Main Street
Waterbury, VT 05671-2901
Phone: 802-241-2158 or 3110
Fax: 802-241-1220
http://www.state.vt.us/srs/childcare/licensing/
license.htm

**Vermont Association of Child Care
Resource and Referral Agencies**
P.O. Box 542
Hinesburg, VT 05461
Phone: 802-482-4400
Fax: 802-482-5446

Vermont Department of Education
Attn.: State Director, Child Nutrition Programs
120 State Street
Montpelier, VT 05602-2702
Phone: 802-828-5154
Fax: 802-828-5107
http://www.state.vt.us/educ/nutrition/

Vermont Office of Child Support
103 South Main Street
Waterbury, VT 05671-1901
Phone: 802-241-2319
Fax: 802-244-1483
http://www.osc.state.vt.us/

U.S. Small Business Administration
87 State Street
Montpelier, VT 05602
Phone: 802-828-4422
Fax: 802-828-4485

To report suspected child abuse in Vermont,
call 802-241-2131 (not toll free).

State Home Page: http://www.state.vt.us/

State Child Care Home Page:
http://www.state.vt.us/srs/childcare/index.htm

Virgin Islands

Virgin Islands Department of Human Services
Knud Hansen Complex Building A
1303 Hospital Ground
Charlotte Amalie, St. Thomas, VI 00802
Phone: 340-774-0930
Fax: 340-774-3466

Department of Human Services
Child Care Licensing
3011 Golden Rock
Christiansted, St. Croix
U.S. Virgin Islands 00820-4355
Phone: 340-773-2323
Fax: 340-773-6121

Department of Education
Attn.: State Director, Child Nutrition Programs
44-46 Kongens Gade
Charlotte Amalie, St. Thomas, VI 00802
Phone: 340-774-9373
Fax: 340-774-9705

Virgin Islands Department of Justice
Paternity and Child Support Division
GERS Building, 2nd Floor
48B-50C Kronprindsens Gade
St. Thomas, VI 00802
Phone: 340-774-4339
Fax: 340-774-9710

To report suspected child abuse in the Virgin Islands, call 1-800-422-4453 (ChildHelp USA).

State Home Page: http://www.usvi.org/

Virginia

Virginia Department of Social Services
Child Day Care
730 E. Broad Street
Richmond, VA 23219-1849
Phone: 804-692-1298
Fax: 804-692-2209
http://www.dss.state.va.us/family/childcare.html

Virginia Department of Social Serv
Child Day Care Programs
Head Start–State Collaboration Offic
730 East Broad Street, 2nd Floor
Richmond, VA 23219-1849
Phone: 804-692-0935
Fax: 804-786-9610
http://www.dss.state.va.us/family/headstartco.h

Department of Social Services
Division of Licensing Programs
730 E. Broad Street, 7th Floor
Richmond, VA 23219-1849
Phone: 804-692-1787 or 1-800-543-7545
Fax: 804-692-2370
http://www.dss.state.va.us/division/license/

Council of Community Services
P.O. Box 598
Roanoke, VA 24004
Phone: 540-985-0131
Fax: 540-982-2935

Virginia Department of Social Services
Division of Child Support Enforcement
730 East Broad Street
Richmond, VA 23219
Phone: 804-692-1501
Fax: 804-692-1543
http://www.dss.state.va.us/division/childsupp/

U.S. Small Business Administration
Federal Building, Suite 1150
400 North 8th Street, Box 10126
Richmond, VA 23240-0126
Phone: 804-771-2400
Fax: 804-771-2764

To report suspected child abuse in Virginia, call 1-800-552-7096.

State Home Page: http://www.state.va.us/

State Child Care Home Page:
http://www.dss.state.va.us/family/childcare.html

...oration Project
...epartment of
...th Services,
...ervices Administration
...of Child Care and Early Learning
. Box 45480
Olympia, WA 98504

Department of Social and Health Services
Office of Child Care Policy
P.O. Box 45700
Olympia, WA 98504
Phone: 360-902-8039
Fax: 360-902-7903
http://www.wa.gov/dshs/occp/license.html

Washington State Child Care
Resource and Referral Network
917 Pacific Avenue, Suite 600
Tacoma, WA 98402-4421
Phone: 253-383-1735
Alt. Phone: 800-446-1114
Fax: 253-572-2599
http://www.childcarenet.org/

Washington Office of Superintendent of
Public Instruction
Attn.: State Director, Child Nutrition Section
Old Capitol Building, 600 South Washington Street
P.O. Box 47200
Olympia, WA 98504-7200
Phone: 360-753-3580
Fax: 360-664-9397
http://www.k12.wa.us/ChildNutrition/

Washington DSHS
Division of Child Support
P.O. Box 9162
Olympia, WA 98507-9162
Phone: 360-586-3520
Fax: 360-586-3274

U.S. Small Business Administration
1200 6th Avenue, Suite 1805
Seattle, WA 98101-1128
Phone: 206-553-5676
Fax: 206-553-2872

To report suspected child abuse in Washington,
call 1-866-End Harm.

State Home Page: http://access.wa.gov/

State Child Care Home Page:
http://www.wa.gov/dshs/occp/index.html

West Virginia

West Virginia Department of
Health and Human Resources
Bureau for Children and Families
Office of Social Services, Division of
Planning Services
350 Capitol Street, Room 691
Charleston, WV 25301-3700
Phone: 304-558-0938
Fax: 304-558-8800

Governor's Cabinet on Children and Families
Head Start–State Collaboration Office
1900 Kanawha Boulevard East
Capitol Complex, Building 5, Room 218
Charleston, WV 25305
Phone: 304-558-4638
Fax: 304-558-0596

Department of Health and Human Resources
Day Care Licensing
P.O. Box 2590
Fairmont, WV 26555-2590
Phone: 304-363-3261
Fax: 304-367-2729
http://www.wvdhhr.org/oss/childcare/licensing.htm
http://www.daycare.com/westvirginia/

River Valley Child Development Services
2850 5th Avenue
Huntington, WV 25702
Phone: 304-523-3417

West Virginia Department of Education
Attn.: State Director, Office of Child Nutrition
Building 6, Room B-248
1900 Kanawha Boulevard East
Charleston, WV 25305-0330
Phone: 304-558-2708
Fax: 304-558-1149

West Virginia Department of
Health and Human Resources
Bureau of Child Support Enforcement
350 Capitol Street, Room 147
Charleston, WV 25305-3703
Phone: 304-558-3780
Fax: 304-558-4092
http://www.wvdhhr.org/bcse/

U.S. Small Business Administration
320 West Pike Street, Suite 330
Clarksburg, WV 26301
Phone: 304-623-5631
Fax: 304-623-4269

To report suspected child abuse in West Virginia, call 1-800-352-6513.

State Home Page: http://www.state.wv.us/

State Child Care Home Page:
http://www.wvdhhr.org/oss/childcare/

Wisconsin

Wisconsin Department of Workforce Development
Office of Child Care
201 East Washington Avenue, Room 171
P.O. Box 7935
Madison, WI 53707-7935
Phone: 608-267-3708
Fax: 608-261-6968
http://www.dwd.state.wi.us/dws/programs/
childcare/default.htm

Wisconsin Department of Workforce Development
Office of Child Care
Head Start–State Collaboration Office
201 E. Washington Avenue
Madison, WI 53707-7935
Phone: 608-261-4596
Fax: 608-267-3240

Division of Children and Family Ser
Bureau of Regulation and Licensing
1 West Wilson Street
P.O. Box 8916
Madison, WI 53708-8916
Phone: 608-266-9314
Fax: 608-267-7252
http://www.dhfs.state.wi.us/rl_dcfs/index.htm

Wisconsin Child Care Resource and Referral
Network, Inc.
519 W. Wisconsin Avenue
Appleton, WI 54911
Phone: 920-734-1739
Fax: 920-734-3887
http://www.wisconsinccrr.org/

Wisconsin Department of Public Instruction
Attn.: State Director, Food and Nutrition Services
125 South Webster Street
P.O. Box 7841
Madison, WI 53707-7841
Phone: 608-267-9121
Fax: 608-267-0363
http://www.dpi.state.wi.us/dpi/dfm/fns/

Wisconsin Division of Economic Support
Bureau of Child Support
P.O. Box 7935
Madison, WI 53707-7935
Phone: 608-266-9909
Fax: 608-267-2824

U.S. Small Business Administration
310 West Wisconsin Avenue, Room 400
Milwaukee, WI 53203
Phone: 414-297-3941
Fax: 414-297-1377

To report suspected child abuse in Wisconsin, call the county Department of Social or Human Services or the local sheriff or police department.

State Home Page:
http://www.wisconsin.gov/state/home/

State Child Care Home Page:
http://www.dwd.state.wi.us/des/childcare/

Wyoming Department of Education
Attn.: State Director, Health and Safety Programs
Hathaway Building, 2nd Floor
2300 Capitol Avenue
Cheyenne, WY 82002-0050
Phone: 307-777-6282
Fax: 307-777-6234
http://www.k12.wy.us/hsandn/index.html

Wyoming Department of Family Services
Child Support Enforcement Program
Hathaway Building, Room 361
2300 Capitol Avenue
Cheyenne, WY 82002-0710
Phone: 307-777-3695
Fax: 307-777-3693

_oration Office
_uite 111
_2
_66-2452
_721-2084
_//wind.uwyo.edu/headstart/

U.S. Small Business Administration
Wyoming District Office
100 East B Street,
Room 4001, Federal Building
P.O. Box 2839
Casper, WY 82602
Phone: 307-261-6500
Toll Free: 1-800-776-9144, Ext. 1
TTY/TDD: 307-261-6527
Fax: 307-261-6535

Department of Family Services
Division of Juvenile Services
Hathaway Building, Room 343
2300 Capitol Avenue
Cheyenne, WY 82002-0490
Phone: 307-777-6285
Fax: 307-777-3659

To report suspected child abuse in Wyoming,
call 1-800-457-3659.

State Home Page: http://www.state.wy.us/

Child Care Finder
c/o Children and Nutrition Services
P.O. Box 2455
800 Werner Court, Suite 185
Casper, WY 82602
Phone: 307-235-7921
Toll Free: 1-800-583-6129
Fax: 307-266-4410
http://www.childrens-nutrition.com/page4.html

State Child Care Home Page:
http://dfsweb.state.wy.us/childcare/toc.htm

Appendix C
Sample Management Forms

Attendance Sheet

CHILD CARE FACILITY: _____ **TEACHER/PROVIDER:** _____

DATE: _____

NAME: _____ TIME IN: _____ TIME OUT: _____

NAME: _____ TIME IN: _____ TIME OUT: _____

NAME: _____ TIME IN: _____ TIME OUT: _____

NAME: _____ TIME IN: _____ TIME OUT: _____

NAME: _____ TIME IN: _____ TIME OUT: _____

NAME: _____ TIME IN: _____ TIME OUT: _____

NAME: _____ TIME IN: _____ TIME OUT: _____

NAME: _____ TIME IN: _____ TIME OUT: _____

NAME: _____ TIME IN: _____ TIME OUT: _____

NAME: _____ TIME IN: _____ TIME OUT: _____

NAME: _____ TIME IN: _____ TIME OUT: _____

NAME: _____ TIME IN: _____ TIME OUT: _____

NAME: _____ TIME IN: _____ TIME OUT: _____

NAME: _____ TIME IN: _____ TIME OUT: _____

NAME: _____ TIME IN: _____ TIME OUT: _____

NAME: _____ TIME IN: _____ TIME OUT: _____

NAME: _____ TIME IN: _____ TIME OUT: _____

NAME: _____ TIME IN: _____ TIME OUT: _____

Back-Up Care Form

LIST OF CHILD CARE FACILITIES THAT PROVIDE SUBSTITUTE CARE:

1. NAME OF FACILITY: _____

CHILD CARE PROVIDER: _____

ADDRESS: _____

PHONE NUMBER: _____

2. NAME OF FACILITY: _____

CHILD CARE PROVIDER: _____

ADDRESS: _____

PHONE NUMBER: _____

3. NAME OF FACILITY: _____

CHILD CARE PROVIDER: _____

ADDRESS: _____

PHONE NUMBER: _____

4. NAME OF FACILITY: _____

CHILD CARE PROVIDER: _____

ADDRESS: _____

PHONE NUMBER: _____

PROVIDER'S NAME AND SIGNATURE: _____

_____

DATE COMPLETED: _____

Child's Development Progress Report

DATE: _____

PROVIDER'S NAME: _____

CHILD'S NAME: _____

AGE: _____

PROGRAM: _____

COMMENTS OR CONCERNS:

_____
_____
_____

CHILD'S INTERESTS:

_____
_____
_____

CHILD'S ABILITIES:

_____
_____
_____

DEVELOPMENTAL GOALS FOR THE CHILD:

_____
_____
_____

SKILLS OR ABILITIES THE CHILD HAS ACQUIRED OR IS WORKING ON:

_____
_____
_____

NEXT REVIEW DATE: _____

Communication Slip

DATE: _____

PROVIDER'S NAME: _____

PROGRAM: _____

CAREGIVER'S COMMENTS:

_____

_____

_____

_____

_____

_____

_____

PARENT'S COMMENTS:

_____

_____

_____

_____

_____

_____

_____

PLAN OF ACTION:

_____

_____

_____

_____

_____

_____

PARENT'S SIGNATURE: _____ DATE: _____

CAREGIVER'S SIGNATURE: _____ DATE: _____

Daily Feedback Sheet

CHILD'S NAME: _____

ROOM: _____

DATE: _____

DIAPER CHANGING: INITIALS

Time:		Asleep	Dry	Wet	Loose	Firm	Provider:
Time:		Asleep	Dry	Wet	Loose	Firm	Provider:
Time:		Asleep	Dry	Wet	Loose	Firm	Provider:
Time:		Asleep	Dry	Wet	Loose	Firm	Provider:
Time:		Asleep	Dry	Wet	Loose	Firm	Provider:

EATING RECORDS:

Time: **Child drank/ate:** _____

Time: **Child drank/ate:** _____

Time: **Child drank/ate:** _____

Time: **Child drank/ate:** _____

SLEEPING RECORDS:

Time: **To**

Time: **To**

Time: **To**

CAREGIVER NOTES OR COMMENTS:

_____

_____

_____

_____

_____

DATE: _____

PROGRAM THE CHILD WILL BE ATTENDING: _____

CHILD'S NAME: _____

AGE: _____

DATE OF BIRTH: _____

ADDRESS: _____

HOME PHONE NUMBER: _____

MOTHER: _____

ADDRESS: _____

HOME PHONE NUMBER: _____

WORK PHONE NUMBER: _____

FATHER: _____

ADDRESS: _____

HOME PHONE NUMBER: _____

WORK PHONE NUMBER: _____

EMERGENCY CONTACT PERSON: _____

ADDRESS: _____

PHONE NUMBER: _____

DATE: _____

LIST OF DESIGNATED PEOPLE FOR PICKUP:

1. _____

2. _____

3. _____

SPECIAL INSTRUCTIONS:

_____

_____

_____

_____

_____

_____

_____

_____

_____

_____

_____

_____

_____

KNOWN ALLERGIES:

_____

_____

_____

_____

_____

_____

_____

_____

_____

Field Trip Consent Form

DATE: _____

AUTHORIZATION

My child, _____ , ( ) does or ( ) does not have my authorization to go to

_____

supervised by _____

on the following date: _____

PARENT OR GUARDIAN: _____

SPECIAL INSTRUCTIONS:

_____

_____

_____

_____

_____

_____

Fire Drill Evacuation Form

ROOM: _____ TEACHER/PROVIDER: _____

DATE	AREA OF SIMULATED FIRE	START TIME	END TIME	EXIT USED	NUMBER OF CHILDREN
5/2/02	Kitchen	9:30	10:05	Front Door	12

Incident Report

CHILD'S NAME: _____

ROOM: _____

DATE: _____

TIME: _____

ACTIVITY PLACE (Place Where the Situation Occurred):

_____

_____

_____

DESCRIPTION OF OCCURRENCE:

_____

_____

_____

NOTIFICATION OF SUPERVISOR:
Yes ( )   No ( )

ACTIONS TAKEN:

_____

_____

_____

SUGGESTED FOLLOW-UP:

_____

_____

_____

STAFF SIGNATURE: _____

DATE: _____TIME:_____

PARENT OR GUARDIAN SIGNATURE: _____

DATE: _____TIME:_____

Medical Consent Form

CHILD'S NAME: _____

DATE OF BIRTH: _____

MOTHER: _____

WORK: _____

ADDRESS: _____

HOME PHONE NUMBER: _____

WORK PHONE NUMBER: _____

FATHER: _____

WORK: _____

ADDRESS: _____

HOME PHONE NUMBER: _____

WORK PHONE NUMBER: _____

PHYSICIAN'S NAME: _____

PHONE NUMBER: _____

IMMUNIZATIONS: _____

_____

SPECIAL INSTRUCTIONS: _____

_____

AUTHORIZATION: _____ has my permission to obtain
(FACILITY NAME)
emergency medical treatment for my child when I cannot be reached or if a delay in reaching my
child will present a dangerous situation for him or her.

PARENT OR GUARDIAN SIGNATURE: _____

DATE: _____

Parent Comment Form

DATE: _____

PARENT'S NAME: _____

CHILD'S NAME: _____

ADDRESS: _____

DESCRIPTION OF THE PROBLEM OR SITUATION:

_____
_____
_____
_____
_____
_____

ACTIONS TAKEN:

_____
_____
_____
_____
_____
_____

PARENT-TEACHER CONFERENCE: YES ( )   NO ( )

DATE: _____

PLACE: _____

NOTES, OBSERVATIONS, OR COMMENTS:

_____
_____
_____
_____

STAFF OR MANAGEMENT: _____

PARENT OR GUARDIAN: _____

Progress Report Form

CHILD'S NAME: _____

ROOM: _____

DATE: _____

TIME: _____

ACTIVITY PLACE:

_____

_____

DESCRIPTION OF OCCURRENCE:

_____

_____

_____

_____

ACTIONS TAKEN:

_____

_____

_____

_____

SUGGESTED FOLLOW-UP:

_____

_____

_____

_____

STAFF SIGNATURE: _____

DATE: _____ TIME: _____

PARENT OR GUARDIAN SIGNATURE: _____

DATE: _____ TIME: _____

Sign In Sheet

CHILD'S NAME: _____

AGE: _____

TIME IN: _____   TIME OUT: _____

CHILD APPEARS HEALTHY UPON ARRIVAL: YES ( )   NO ( )

COMMENTS:

_____

_____

_____

_____

TIME CHILD NAPPED: _____

TIME CHILD AWOKE: _____

CHILD'S LAST FEEDING: _____

FEEDING SCHEDULE: _____

SUPPLIES PROVIDED:

_____

_____

_____

SPECIAL INSTRUCTIONS:

_____

_____

_____

_____

SPECIAL NOTES OR COMMENTS:

_____

_____

_____

_____

Index